Germany Travel Guide
I love Germany

By S. L. Giger as *SwissMiss on Tour*

"Nothing develops intelligence like travel."
– Emile Zola

Self-published. Contact: Seraina Cavalli,
swissmissontour@gmail.com
Cover design: Seraina Cavalli
Cover pictures: Rachel Davis on Unsplash (Neuschwanstein),
Roman Kraft on Unsplash (Rothenburg ob der Tauber), Franz
Kowiaka on Pixabay (Tiger and Turtle)

Receive a free packing list

Never forget anything important ever again and don't waste unnecessary time with packing. Scan the QR code and receive a free packing list along with a sample of my Thailand travel guide.

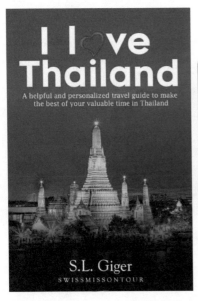

Germany travel guide

Why should I choose this Germany travel guide instead of another?

Do you only have a limited amount of time (for example, two or three weeks) and feel a little overwhelmed about which places to visit in Germany? Should it be the metropolises of Berlin or Munich? Or would you prefer smaller, picturesque towns or castles? Germany offers a wide range of breathtaking places. Therefore, it can be difficult to decide on a route. This guide will help you to focus on Germany's top sights. Explore the Reichstag or the Wall, walk along Germany's beautiful rivers, browse historic cities like Cologne and Dresden, and sample specialties from all parts of the country. In addition, *I love Germany* introduces you to other great sights and activities along the highlights route so that you have a colorful program. Even as a local or as a visitor from a neighboring country, you will still be amazed by the many treasures of Germany.

With *I love Germany* you don't have to do any further travel research. You will find a two-week itinerary with detailed instructions and further ideas and descriptions compact in this book. Save time and enjoy the anticipation completely.

Admire medieval half-timbered houses, cities that have perfectly integrated rivers or streams into urban planning, see fairytale castles, and learn about Germany's history.

Do you want to plan your trip to Germany stress-free and travel safely? Then this travel guide is the right one for you. It provides all the information you need to plan and execute a smooth trip. From the best itinerary to local attractions to practical tips on the go; everything you need is included here.

If you are worried about the German language, there is a list with helpful vocabulary at the end of this book. However, since most Germans younger than 35 learned English at school, you'll be fine with English, hands, feet, and Google Translate.

Reasons to look forward to your trip to Germany if you are not entirely convinced yet

Even if you've already been to Germany, you will agree that it is always a great idea to explore Germany as a tourist and enjoy its many fantastic sights, culinary delights, and wonderful experiences!

I'm from Switzerland and I am often drawn to exotic countries far away. That's why I have to admit that an extended trip to Germany was not my first priority. However, I am positively surprised every time I visit Germany and always find new treasures, no matter where I go. The additional trips for this travel guide opened my eyes even more, to what there still is to discover in Germany. From now on, I will certainly be drawn to our big neighbor more often. Fortunately, I am in Constance in 40 minutes by train and can enjoy this pretty city as well as the other places worth seeing along Lake Constance. Even this small part of Germany convinces me to come back again and again.

Another reason why I like to visit Germany is that all the cuisines of the world are represented in the big cities. Above all, you will also find many modern vegetarian and vegan restaurants with refined dishes.

In addition, there are so many more reasons to look forward to your trip to Germany! Discover time-honored churches, castles, palaces, and more! There are also many opportunities to explore Germany's rich history, whether through the traces of German unification or World War II.

The landscape is also impressive and shows a variety of contrasts: Whether it is the peaks of the Alps, the wide river valleys of the blue Rhine, or the beaches of northern

Photo: Lüneburg Heath

Germany – everyone will find something to their taste here. And if you then follow the cycling or hiking trails along the Main or Rhine, you can really relax!

So, now it's your turn. Read what there is to see in Germany and enjoy an unforgettable time!

The highlights of Germany

I say it again and again, but it also applies to Germany; there are so many highlights that it is very difficult to pick the best of the best. So here are my three highlights from the field of architecture.

1 Reichstag in Berlin

The building with its gleaming glass dome looks remarkable from the outside. The great thing is that you can visit the dome on a spiral path along the glass window front. Thus, the Reichstag is not only an important political building but also an attractive sight.

2 Fischerviertel in Ulm

There are many beautiful medieval buildings in Germany and the number of towns or villages worth mentioning is huge. For example, the Römerhof in Frankfurt is also a place worth seeing if you like half-timbered houses. However, the fishing quarter in Ulm is particularly charming, as, in addition to the very pretty half-timbered houses, a stream flows between the buildings. Plus, the cobblestone streets are connected by small bridges. Simply a welcoming place for a walk.

3 Neuschwanstein

There are many beautiful castles in the world, but this one is especially romantic (from the outside at least). In addition, you can enjoy the hilly and green landscape of Bavaria.

Things to consider before visiting Germany to have the best trip possible

Here are the things you need to know to have a smooth trip.

Currency

Germany uses the euro. The short form is EUR or €. At the time of writing this book, 1 USD was equivalent to 0.95 EUR. You can find the current exchange rate by typing "USD to EUR" into the Google search bar.

Almost everywhere you can also pay by debit card or credit card, except perhaps at a vegetable stall. There it is good if you have some cash with you.

Best time to visit Germany

Since it can also be rainy or cold in Germany, you have the best chance of sunny weather in the summer months of June, July, and August. Then the climate in Germany is usually very pleasant and warm and ideal for exploring different cities and areas. In addition, many beach bars come to life in Germany in summer. When temperatures climb over 30 degrees, the many rivers and lakes invite you for a swim.

Even in spring and autumn, temperatures can be pleasant, although it might be a bit rainier.

The winter months are often cold and it gets dark early. Then it is best to bring a down jacket, hat, and gloves. However, there are many romantic Christmas markets in December, which attract thousands of tourists and locals every year.

Federal states

Germany consists of 16 federal states. The main government has its offices in Berlin and Bonn. However, the 16 federal states can set some individual rules, which is why, for example, you don't have the same holidays everywhere or the Covid regulations were different from state to state as well. Here you have an overview of the federal states.

Vaccinations and Visas

For Germany, it is recommended that you have the routine vaccines like MMR, Diphtheria-Tetanus-Pertussis, Polio, etc. but nothing is mandatory.

New ETIAS Visa

Up to now, most countries could enter Germany and the Schengen area without a visa for up to 90 days. However, that changes in 2025, when most countries that don't belong to the EU or Schengen area will have to buy an ETIAS Visa before coming to the Schengen area. It's a quick online authorization, similar to the ESTA that you need for the US.

Check on this website (www.schengenvisa-info.com/etias/who-needs-etias/) whether your nationality will need an ETIAS Visa or whether your country already needs a normal visa now (for example India, China, or South Africa).

Covid regulations

Germany has always been much stricter with lockdowns and mandatory masks than Switzerland and would therefore probably reintroduce measures more quickly. Therefore, it is all the more important that you check the current situation before you travel to Germany. Since everything is changing so quickly when it comes to Covid, I can't give you current travel advice for that. At the moment of writing this, everything is good and I really hope that it will still be the case when you read this book. However, if Covid regulations are back in place, you should check the following:

1. What regulations do the individual federal states currently have in Germany? Can your nationality enter Germany? Do you need proof of a test, recovery, or vaccination?

You can check the current requirements for Germany on this website: www.bundesregierung.de/breg-de/themen/coronavirus/

2. Are there any obligations when returning to your country?
You may need to take an antigen test or a PCR test and maybe Germany is on your country's quarantine list. In Germany, it was very easy to get tested. Improvised test centers have popped up everywhere.

3. Do you need a test or vaccination for the airline you're flying with or because of the stopover you have?
If you have any questions about this, it is best to contact the airline for information.

Drinking water

Tap water in Germany can be drunk without hesitation. There are strict norms and standards for the quality of water. In addition, the purity of the water is regularly tested. Therefore, it is best to bring your personal water bottle to save plastic and not have

to buy drinks all the time. Simply fill your bottle with water from the tap.

How to find the right way

Like everywhere I go, I've used the **maps.me app** on my phone and downloaded Germany for offline use. This was a very useful companion every day and always took me to the place I wanted to go. You can use maps.me to find points of interest within a city, to get to your accommodation, or to follow a hiking route (e.g. in Saxon Switzerland). Tourists can mark places and write comments. So, you can even discover secret spots that other tourists recommend.

Wi-Fi

All our accommodations and many restaurants, cafés, and shopping centers offered free Wi-Fi. In addition, some express trains of the *Deutsche Bahn* had well-functioning Wi-Fi.

How to choose your accommodation

Since travelers all have their own preferences about how their accommodation should be, I hardly include recommendations for hostels or hotels in my travel guides. The best deals for Germany you can find on **booking.com** if you reached Genius level. There you also have the latest reviews for the accommodation, and you can get different opinions about a place before you arrive. Otherwise, you get the best hostel and hotel deals if you book directly on the website of the accommodation.

If you only have a tight budget, you could try Couchsurfing or **Airbnb**.

With the Interrail Pass, you have a discount in some hostels.

Book your accommodation through me

Since recently, I have access to the booking platforms, with which travel agencies work. That's why I could find better hotel deals for you. If you are interested, send me an e-mail (swiss-missontour@gmail.com) with the dates and your desired hotel (with or without breakfast?) or the desired city and your budget and I can check the price for you or book your nights directly. However, I have noticed that it is more worthwhile for 4- or 5-star hotels. The cheaper hotels have such a small margin that the prices on the hotel website or

Booking.com are sometimes the same or cheaper than the prices on the business booking platforms.

Introductory offer: If you book three or more nights through me, I will send you another travel guide (of mine) of your choice free of charge as an e-book. This applies to hotel bookings around the world.

Learn German

In Germany, it is not necessary to speak German in order to travel. The locals are used to tourists and often speak English, Dutch, or French. Nevertheless, it has a great effect on the locals if you utter the first words you say to them in German. They will appreciate your effort and you will quickly become friends.

If you want to learn German, you could start with the free **Duolingo app**. However, I think there is so much unnecessary vocabulary that you just don't need on a trip. Then, **busuu** or **Babel** are the better choices. First, you take a test that will allow you to start learning exactly at your German level. The way it is set up makes the words and grammar sink in well. You need to buy the premium program to be able to access all the courses. This is much cheaper than a German course at a school and you can study while sitting on a plane or train.

In addition, you will find a small list of German travel vocabulary at the end of this book.

Tips on how to travel cheaply to and in Germany

If you are already in Europe, you might be able to travel to Germany by train. *Deutsche Bahn* regularly offers international and national saver tickets, whereby you can travel throughout the country for 9 to 35 EUR. So it's really worth taking a look at the website of the Deutsche Bahn first (www.bahn.de).

If you don't have that much time to cross Germany by train (which can easily take 8 hours), you can find flight bargains with **Ryanair**. If Ryanair doesn't fly to your airport, you can use the following tips to search for cheap flight tickets.

1. Use multiple flight search engines

I usually start with **Sky Scanner** and then compare the

deals on **CheapTickets** and/or **Opodo**. These sites usually offer the cheapest prices. With Sky Scanner you can set a price alert that informs you by e-mail if there are cheaper flights. You could start this half a year before your trip.

Another option is to type the flight directly into Google to get an approximate estimate of what the airfare will be. In the end, I always look on the websites of the cheapest airlines for special offers. For Germany, these are EasyJet and Ryanair.

2. Be early and buy your plane ticket at least 3 months in advance

If you know the dates of your holiday, there is no reason to wait to book your flights. They are just getting more expensive.

However, in times of Covid, where everything is so uncertain, you're probably better off booking last minute. It's not necessarily cheap, but otherwise, you may have to cancel your vacation if a country suddenly closes its borders.

3. Be a little flexible

Also check the dates three days before and after the dates you have selected for the flight. It could make a big price difference! If you search on CheapTickets or Sky Scanner, it is very easy to get an overview of the flight prices on different dates.

4. Look at all potential airports

Germany has many large, international airports. Munich, Frankfurt, and Dusseldorf are usually the cheapest to fly to, and depending on your itinerary you can start or end your trip in another city.

5. Delete your browsing history

The websites where you searched for your flight tickets to Germany will recognize you on your second visit. Then they raise the prices a little bit because you're still interested. So, if you notice a price increase, the first thing you should do is close the website and then delete your browsing history. After that, you only look again when you are ready to book. It's amazing how quickly you can save money this way.

6. Sign up for the newsletter of your favorite airlines

Newsletters still offer added value and often you will find special offers on airline tickets in them. At the moment I regularly receive special offers from TUI and Swiss. By the way, *SwissMiss OnTour* also offers a newsletter. Sign up on www.swissmissontour.com to get my latest blog posts and a free, helpful packing list.

7. Fly with carry-on baggage only

If you're going on a city-hopping trip, you don't want to carry too much weight around with you anyway. If you only pack the essentials, it fits in a backpack well. You protect your wallet and your back, as the maximum weight for the allowed carry-on luggage is between 8 and 10 kg per person. Unfortunately, you have to do without big shopping tours.

Important German festivals and traditions

In Germany, the usual Christian holidays such as Christmas and Easter are celebrated. That's why Germany is also worth a visit between the end of November and Christmas when many cities are enriched by Christmas markets. It smells of gingerbread, waffles, and chocolate fruits. Or would you rather treat yourself to a mulled wine, a Feuerzangenbowle, or a delicious sausage? The agony of choice makes your mouth water, and you can easily visit several Christmas markets.

In addition to the Christmas markets, plenty other occasions could influence your trip.

Epiphany

Epiphany (6 January) is a public holiday in three federal states. Then, the shops and many restaurants in Baden-Württemberg, Bavaria, and Saxony-Anhalt are closed. It is the day on which the wise men from the East celebrated the birth of Jesus Christ. The Germans celebrate with cakes, gifts, and songs.

Carnival

Carnival is a large folk festival that takes place every year in February. In different parts of Germany, you can find different forms of carnival. You can look forward to many days full of music, costumes, and jokes!
The largest carnival parade takes place on Shrove Monday in Cologne.

Oktoberfest

This festival, on the other hand, draws guests from all over the world to beer and pretzels. Oktoberfest is one of the largest festivals in Europe and attracts over six million visitors to Munich every year in **mid to late September**. It has existed since 1810. Today there are over 15 large beer tents as well as a fair with rollercoaster rides and food stalls.

Most of the restaurants in the city are festively decorated and you can eat and drink Munich specialties everywhere. Most men come in lederhosen and the women in a dirndl. Don't worry, if you don't have the right outfit yet, in the shops in Munich you will certainly find something suitable.

Labor Day

Labor Day (1 May) is still actively used in Germany to reinforce demands for fair working conditions. There are speech duels, slogans, and demonstrations, which are not always peaceful. Depending on this, you should better avoid these events

Traveling by train and bus – public transport in Germany

Public transport in Germany is good, as there is a network of connections that run through the whole country. In addition, the trains are comfortable and *Deutsche* *Bahn* often offers fantastic promotions (as already mentioned in the chapter on cheap travel).

The disadvantage is that there are many delays, which makes planning difficult. It is not worthwhile to select connections on which you have to change trains, as you usually don't catch the connection. If this is your only option, it is therefore not advisable to reserve a seat on the express trains, as you will usually end up sitting on a different train anyway (this was my experience at least).

In order to use public transport as efficiently as possible, I suggest downloading the *Deutsche Bahn* app and buying all tickets directly in the app or looking up connections in the app's timetable planner.

Traveling by rental car in Germany

In Germany, a long list of well-known car brands is produced. With so much car enthusiasm, of course, the road network is also well developed. On the motorways there often is no speed limit and you can drive as fast as the road safety is still guaranteed. The positive thing about traveling by car in Germany is that you can cover a lot of ground (unless you are stopped at one of the countless construction sites) and you are not bound by the travel times of public transport. In addition, you can load the luggage comfortably into the car and do not have to carry it around.

The downside is that navigating cities is always a bit more complicated than overland. In addition, with such a good public transport network, you are not dependent on the car in cities. However, I must say that it is still easier to find a parking space in German cities than in other European countries.

If you don't arrive with your own car, it is easy to reserve a car online in advance with one of the countless car rental companies (Hertz, Sixt, Europcar, etc.) and pick it up at your desired starting point. On www.billiger-mietwagen.de, all offers are compared.

Traveling in Germany with children

Since Germany is a very safe travel destination, you can well visit it with the whole family. In addition to the attractions for adults, there are also many parks, museums, zoos, amusement parks, water activities, and playgrounds that make children's eyes shine.

In the Müller or DM, you will also find everything you need for a baby in good quality and at reasonable prices (milk formula, diapers, ready-made porridge, etc.).

However, if you are traveling with a stroller, you should think twice about a trip to Germany. Most cities in Germany are not yet very stroller friendly. There rarely are functioning elevators at the train stations and the trains or trams are often only accessible via a staircase.

In addition, many buildings are not barrier-free. Often, you need to walk a detour with the stroller until you finally arrive where you want to go. This makes sightseeing quite exhausting, as you are already traveling a lot on foot anyway. Hence you will always be dependent on the help of strangers to get the stroller up and down the stairs. If you aren't shy, however, this is not a problem and you will quickly be surprised by how friendly and helpful the Germans are.

Unfortunately, it is a different matter for restaurants or hotels. There, I often noticed a dislike of the staff as soon as they saw me with the stroller. That is a pity. In Italy, Spain, or Greece, I generally received a friendlier welcome.

Typical German food and drinks you need to try

When you think of Spain, Thailand, or Mexico, you automatically think of several typical dishes that you treated yourself to on your last holiday or that you order again and again in the restaurant. In Germany, there are also two specialties for which I am very grateful that they were invented in Germany (pretzel) and perfected in Germany (beer). In this list, you will find some more dishes that you will certainly encounter in Germany.

- **White sausages**

Speaking of a pretzel, of course, some white sausages also go with it. The tender sausages are heated in hot water. Then you peel off their skin and dip them into sweet mustard. In Germany, white sausages are mainly served for breakfast, but you can of course also enjoy them as a snack with a beer. After all, there are so many good beer brands in Germany that you have to start tasting them right away.

- **Sauerkraut**

This cabbage dish is often served as an accompaniment to meat and potatoes. When done well, it is very healthy for the body. If it's not the best quality, it retains its laxative effect and hopefully, you have a room with a private toilet ;).

- **Potato salad**

A feel-good dish with a delicious sauce, which goes well with many German dishes as a side or can be enjoyed as a main meal with a slice of bread.

- **Bockwurst and other sausages**

The light brown Bockwurst can be found everywhere in Germany. If you prefer a more intense taste, you can try many other types of sausage, whether fried, smoked, or raw (Mettwurst).

- **Käsespätzle**

These flakes of flour, egg, and milk taste especially good when they are gratinated with cheese and sprinkled with roasted onions. After a big portion of spaetzle, you will surely be full and have a good base for long party nights.

- **Dampfnudeln (steamed noodles)**

No, this is not Italian pasta. If you have a sweet tooth, you should try these delicious yeast dough balls with vanilla sauce.

The most beautiful half-timbered houses in Germany

Since I first visited the big cities of Germany, I did not realize how many idyllic corners Germany has to offer. You often feel like you're in a fairy tale. The most romantic places are **Rothenburg ob der Tauber, Quedlinburg**, **Lüneburg,** and **Bamberg**. However, these small places are not all easy to reach by public transport. If you are not cycling on the Romantic Route, it will cost you a lot of time, for example, to get to Rothenburg ob der Tauber.

In the end, however, I came to the conclusion that certain small towns simply market their half-timbered houses better to attract tourists.

So, my favorites among the most beautiful half-timbered houses are namely the **Fischerviertel in Ulm** and the **Römerberg in Frankfurt** (photo). Furthermore, you will come across beautiful half-timbered houses in almost every place in Germany and you do not have to worry about missing something if not every small town fits into your itinerary. It's best to just keep your eyes open everywhere.

Two-week itinerary to experience the best of culture and nature

Since many small towns in Germany also offer true treasures to look at, the following itinerary is just one possible suggestion of countless travel options. With this itinerary, you can visit all the most famous cities and sights and if you have more time, plan some stops in smaller places.

Day 1: Munich

We start our journey with a refreshing beer and other Munich specialties at the Viktualienmarkt. Afterward, a stroll through the old town

and a visit to an art museum or the Bavaria statue is worthwhile.

Day 2: Neuschwanstein Castle

You take a day trip to Neuschwanstein Castle. The rest of the day you can visit everything in Munich that you didn't manage yesterday.

Day 3: Ulm

We continue to Ulm. Once there, you climb the highest church tower in the world to get an overview of the city.

Afterward, you walk through the fishermen's quarter, where you can see beautiful half-timbered houses. From the city wall, you can enjoy more beautiful views and maybe you will have time for the current exhibition at the Kunstverein Ulm.

Day 4: Stuttgart

In Stuttgart, you will visit the Mercedes or Porsche Car Museum, enjoy a leisurely walk through the city and marvel at the architecture in the library.

Day 5: Frankfurt

Frankfurt is a contrast between modern and historic, which is why it is worth exploring the city on foot or taking a leisurely boat trip on the Main.

(If you want to shorten your trip by a day or stay somewhere else, Frankfurt is the stop I would most likely cut out.)

Day 6: Cologne

Here, of course, you greet the cathedral and cross one of the beautiful bridges, from where you can enjoy a different view of the city. A walk along the Rhine is also worthwhile and maybe you still have time for the great Museum Ludwig.

Day 7: Düsseldorf and Duisburg

In Dusseldorf you can fill your belly with Asian food in Little Tokyo, stroll through the old town and enjoy the view from the Rhine Tower. However, you will spend half the day on a trip to the Tiger & Turtle roller coaster sculpture in Duisburg. It's really worth taking the journey to this spectacular walk-in work of art.

Day 8: Hamburg

The journey from Düsseldorf to Hamburg by train takes approx. 3.5h. So take a snack with you, sit back, and look at the passing cities and landscapes from the train window. Once in Hamburg, there is so much to visit, be it a market in St. Pauli or the Speicherstadt.

Therefore, we need at least two days in Hamburg.

Day 9: Hamburg

Take a ride on the public ships on the Elbe and marvel at the great buildings in Hamburg. Maybe you also have time to watch a musical.

Day 10: Lüneburg and Hamburg

Take a trip to the pretty town of Lüneburg today. Check out the historic buildings and half-timbered houses before you have another chance to visit

other places in this fabulous city of Hamburg. Since you have three mornings in Hamburg, hopefully, one of them falls on a Sunday so that you can visit the fish market.

Day 11: Berlin

Today you leave Hamburg and reach Germany's capital. Reserve your visit to the Reichstag building so you can see this fascinating dome today or tomorrow and walk along the East Side Gallery. Don't miss the chance to try out Berlin's diverse nightlife, whether it's with a drink to round off the day or party the night away in a club.

Day 12: Berlin

Check out all the sights in the city center. The sights range from the Brandenburg Gate to the Holocaust Memorial and Checkpoint Charlie.

Day 13: Dresden

Dresden is teeming with beautiful, historic buildings, all of which you can see on foot. In between, you can relax in the *Grosser Garten* or in the garden of the *Zwinger* or enjoy the view from the *Brühlsche Terrasse*.

If you can't extend your trip, you'll fly back home from Dresden or Berlin on day 14 (or take a night train if you live in Europe?). It is worth checking from which city the departure is cheaper. Otherwise, you will continue the program as follows to visit the last highlights and close the circle in Munich.

Day 14: Saxon Switzerland

Take a day trip from Dresden so you can explore the beautiful nature of Saxon Switzerland. You start at the main attraction, the Bastei Bridge, but you can extend your stay with picturesque hikes.

Day 15: Bamberg and Nuremberg

Today, you should get up early. Now, you start your way back south. In three hours, you get from Dresden to Bamberg, where you can see the famous town hall on the bridge. After a city tour, on which you absolutely have to climb the hill with the cathedral, you take the next train to Nuremberg. You will reach this city in 35 minutes. Hopefully, you still have energy, because Nuremberg is also worth exploring on foot and treating yourself to a vegan Asian meal.

Day 16: Return home

If you have traveled to Germany by train, you can start your journey home directly from Nuremberg. Otherwise, you ride to Munich Airport, from where you can fly home. Thus, the circle of your round trip in Germany is closed, but you are probably already thinking about when you can return to Germany next. Then, it might be a different kind of journey, on which you, for example, tackle a bike path or long-distance hiking trail.

This is one possible two-week itinerary that will allow you to see all the highlights in Germany. Now let's take a closer look at the individual places.

Berlin

With its vibrant culture, rich history, and fascinating architecture, Berlin attracts tourists from all over the world. Whether you're looking for wild nightlife or want to see the world-famous cultural sights, Germany's vibrant capital has something for everyone. Put on your most comfortable shoes so that you can visit all the highlights on your sightseeing tour through the city!

From the airport to the city center

Berlin Brandenburg International Airport (BER) is about 30 km from the city center. It has replaced Berlin Tegel and Schönfeld airports. The cheapest and easiest way to get to the city center is by train. Various trains circulate between the station at Terminals 1 and 2 and the main station. The journey takes 30 minutes and costs 3.80 EUR. The S-Bahn lines 9 and S45 cost the same

but take an hour as they stop at several stops. A taxi costs around 55 EUR and takes about 45 minutes. An UBER is only slightly cheaper.

Public transport within the city

Berlin is divided into three zones. Zone A covers the S-Bahn ring. A short trip costs 2 EUR. Zone B ends at Berlin's city limits and a trip in zone AB costs 3 EUR. A 24-hour ticket for 8.80 EUR can quickly become worthwhile. If you also want to see zone C (BER airport or Potsdam), the 24-hour ticket for zone ABC for 10 EUR is a good bargain. A 24h ticket for a small group is a good deal starting at 3 people because it costs only 26.50 EUR (ABC). So, the whole of Berlin is waiting to be explored by you.

Things to do in Berlin

Berlin has so much to offer, be it great shopping, fascinating buildings, and good museums, that you don't really know where to start. That's why I've divided the sights of Berlin into thematic areas. To get an overview, a free walking tour is always a good idea. The tour starts daily at 11 a.m. at Starbucks at the Brandenburg Gate and you can visit Checkpoint Charlie and the Holocaust Memorial. If you prefer it more comfortable, you can also choose one of the following bus rides by public bus.

Take a tour by public bus

Since Berlin is too big to visit everything on foot, you can also just sit back in the public bus 100, 200, or 300 and look at the sights through the window or get off in between. For bus 100 you get on at *Alexanderplatz* and see the *TV tower*. Furthermore, it drives past the *Museum Island*, the *Lustgarten,* the *Brandenburg Gate,* and the *Reichstag*. Continue via *Bellevue Palace* and the *Victory Column* to the *Kaiser Wilhelm Memorial Church*, *Kurfürstendamm,* and the famous *KaDeWe*. The journey ends at *Bahnhof Zoo*.

Bus 200 also starts at *Alexanderplatz,* but also passes *Checkpoint Charlie* and the *Rotes Rathaus.*

Bus 300 takes you from the *Philharmonie* via *Potsdamer Platz* past the *Mall of Berlin* and the *Staatsoper* to the *East Side Gallery*.

Visit the relics of WW2

Since we should learn a lot from the Second World War so that something like this never happens again, many remnants and memorials are still visible in Germany's capital today.

Let's start at the **Holocaust Memorial**, which is located in the heart of Berlin. It offers visitors a haunting reminder of the millions of innocent victims of the Holocaust. The complex consists of more than 2700 concrete blocks, arranged at regular intervals, representing the size ratio of the victims of the Holocaust. Each pillar represents a person

we should not forget. The sight is shocking but also offers great photo opportunities.

Checkpoint Charlie was a border crossing between East and West Berlin during the division of Germany. The checkpoint was opened in 1961 and until reunification served as one of three border crossings where visitors from the West could travel to East Berlin. The customs house of Checkpoint Charlie still stands today, and you can walk past it.

A good, free museum is the **Topography of Terror** (www.topographie.de). The museum is located on the grounds of the former State Security Service of the GDR (SED) and SS in Berlin. It includes exhibits, documents, and artifacts documenting the history of the regime.

Another stop is the **Kaiser Wilhelm Memorial Church**. It symbolizes the destruction caused by the Second World War because the façade of the church still shows the bomb damage as a silent reminder of the terrible events during the war.

The most colorful reminder of the war is the **East Side Gallery**. It is a 1.3 km long open-air gallery at the Berlin Wall, making it the longest surviving piece of the Berlin Wall. The gallery displays more than 105 original street art paintings by artists from around the world. Each mural tells its own story about Berlin's past and present.

If you have plenty of time, you can follow the **Berlin Wall Trail**. The historic Wall Hiking Trail stretches over 155 km and offers insights into the German history of the 20th century. As you walk along the path, you can not only catch a glimpse of the famous Berlin Wall but also stop at many other places and learn more about Berlin's political history.

Visit Berlin's most impressive buildings

As one of Berlin's best-known landmarks, the **Reichstag** is a must-see for any visitor to the city. Opened in 1894, the glass palace houses the parliament of Germany. Plan ahead and sign up for a free visit to the imposing dome. You can book your free time slot here: https://visite.bundes-tag.de/BAPWeb/pages/createBookingRequest/view-BasicInformation.jsf. The tour of the glass dome on the roof terrace itself is spectacular and the view over the Tiergarten and the center of Berlin is just a bonus. Make sure you have your ID or passport with you when you arrive at the Reichstag building at the specified time from your email confirmation.

The **Brandenburg Gate** stands on Pariser Platz and is part of the UNESCO World Heritage Site. Originally built in the 18th century, the archway became a symbol of the reunification of Germany and Europe as a whole after World War II. On New Year's Eve, a big New Year's party with fireworks takes place here.

Alexanderplatz is located in the heart of the city and is one of the largest public squares in Europe. Here you will find numerous shops, bars, and restaurants. In addition, the 368 m high **television tower** stands here. Tickets booked online for the observation deck are available for adults from 22.50 EUR (https://tv-turm.de/online-tickets). A popular photo motif is the **world clock**. The clock was placed in 1969 to symbolize global time and international peace. The dial has 24 fields that are representative of each time zone in the world and indicate the respective time.

Another good and cheaper view can be enjoyed from the 126-meter-high platform of the **radio tower** (8 EUR). It looks a bit like a slimmer version of the Eiffel Tower.

Another great and free view is the **Marzahn Glass Skywalk** above the Marzahn promenade. For the Skywalk you simply have to register for a free guided tour under zkb@degewo.de or call 030-2685-5000. Note the opening hours, which are only a few hours per day (https://Dein-marzahn-hellersdorf.ber-lin/skywalk/).

Finally, the climb to the top of the imposing **Berlin Cathedral** is also worthwhile. The domed terrace is included in the entrance ticket to the cathedral (9 EUR).

More buildings that you have to see from the outside in Berlin are the modern **Philharmonie,** the **State Opera,** and the **Red Town Hall**.

Finally, you could climb the 285 steps to the **Siegessäule** (4 EUR). The Victory Column was erected in 1873 to commemorate the Prussian victories in the German-Danish War and other Prussian successes. Once at the top, you are rewarded with a magnificent view of everything Berlin has to offer! The column is also worth a photo from below.

Just outside the center is the beautiful **Schloss Charlottenburg**. The castle houses the largest collection of royal rooms and works of art in all of Germany. In the castle garden, visitors will find a variety of sculptures, grottos, pavilions, and fountains. A special highlight is the large Pergamon Museum in the castle park. The entrance fee for the whole castle and the castle garden is 19 EUR.

Go shopping or stroll through a market

After so much sightseeing, it's time to sit down in a café or grab a bite to eat at a market stall. Maybe you'll have new energy to browse Berlin's big shopping malls.

A beautiful market hall with local specialties and catering facilities is the **Arminiusmarkthalle** (Arminiusstraße 2-4, mostly open from 12-10 p.m.). The **Schillermarkt** takes place outdoors in Neukölln on Wednesdays from 12 – 7 p.m. and Saturdays from 10 a.m. – 4 p.m.

A great shopping center is the **Mall of Berlin** with over 200 shops and huge glass facades that reflect light reflections.

The **KaDeWe** (Kaufhaus des Westens) is probably the most exclusive shopping center in Berlin. It offers extravagant shops and restaurants, beautiful views over Berlin, and a wide range of international brands.

Germany's largest Asian market, the **Dong Xuan Center**, offers a slightly different shopping experience. With the tram lines M8 and 21 you can get there directly.

Learn something in a museum

The center for museum lovers is, of course, Berlin's **Museum Island**. It is located in the middle of the Spree and is home to five important museums in Berlin (Altes Museum, Neues Museum, Alte Nationalgalerie, Bode Museum, and Pergamonmuseum). Art lovers can enjoy works by Michelangelo, Rembrandt, and Monet, as well as extensive collections of prehistoric art. A visit is worthwhile, even without going to the museums because Museum Island is recognized as a UNESCO World Heritage Site. The day ticket for all museums costs 19 EUR, but for those under 18-years-old, it is free. On the first Sunday of the month, the museums are free for everyone.

If you prefer to search for **street art**, you should stroll through **Kreuzberg**. Treat yourself to a drink in a bar on *Oberbaumstraße* and stroll along the Spree in the *RAW* area. Kreuzberg is also home to many contemporary art galleries as well as creative boutiques and design shops. You can also admire murals at **Haus Schwarzenberg** (Rosenthaler Straße 39).

Breathe fresh air in a park

The **Tempelhofer Feld** is an extensive leisure area, which was opened on the site of the former Berlin-Tempelhof airport. Whether cycling (you could also rent a bike to get around faster), jogging, skateboarding, or walking, Tempelhofer Feld is the perfect place to break out of city life. It also has barbecue areas and countless playgrounds. Two great playgrounds are the dragon playground (Schreinerstraße 48) and the witches' playground (Eisenacher Str. 29).

The **Gardens of the World** (www.gaertenderwelt.de) cost 7 or 4 EUR admission (summer/winter), but since they offer such varied and beautifully designed theme regions, a visit is always a good idea.

Party until the sky turns light again

Berlin offers countless possibilities for partying until dawn. **Berghain** is one of the most famous and popular techno clubs in Berlin. This club is located in the former power station of Berlin and offers a breathtaking atmosphere with its impressive interior. **Watergate** is another famous electro club in Berlin, which is currently known for its innovative DJing and attracts guests from all over the world. The **Club der Visionäre** is mainly known for outdoor parties on the banks of the Spree canal. **Klunkerkranich** is probably the most famous rooftop bar in Berlin (Karl-Marx-Straße 66). Enjoy good drinks, music, and a beautiful view in this open-air bar.

If you want to dance **salsa**, you will enjoy yourself in **Havana Berlin**, in **Clärchens Ballhaus,** or in **Monbijou Park** (outdoors during summer).

Where to eat in Berlin

Those with a sweet tooth will feel at home in the **Rausch Schokoladenhaus**. Fabulous vegan donuts can be found at **Brammibal's Donuts**.

There are countless Kebap shops in Berlin, but one of the most famous is **NUR Gemüse Kebap** (Hermannstraße 113a).

They also have many vegetarian variations.

If your mouth is watering if you think of Mexican food, **Santa Maria** (www.santaberlin.com/) is a good address. On Tuesdays, they offer tacos for 2 EUR.

Take a trip to Potsdam

Several trains per hour run between Berlin and Potsdam (in about 30 minutes, from 3.80 EUR). Since it is still more than 2 kilometers on foot from the main station to the park with the castles, it is best to rent a bike (e.g., at one of the *Nextbike* rental stations). Or you can drive directly from Berlin to *Potsdam Park, Sanssouci* station, where you arrive 500 meters from two castles.

Highlights include the **New Palace,** one of the largest Baroque palaces in Europe, as well as other palaces and parks, all of which are UNESCO World Heritage Sites. **Sanssouci Park** is one of the most famous gardens in Germany and offers visitors a wide range of summer and winter attractions. The park was laid out in the 18th century by Frederick the Great, King of Prussia, and today visitors can marvel at the magnificent

Sanssouci Palace and the extensive grounds with their ponds and meadows.

On the way back, you should definitely stop by the **Dutch Quarter** in the city center of Potsdam and take a break in a café or restaurant. This district consists of beautiful, red brick houses, which King Frederick William I had built by Dutch craftsmen in the mid-1700s. Fortunately, Potsdam recognized the potential of these houses and had them renovated in 1990 so that an inviting neighborhood could be created.

Dresden

Dresden was heavily damaged during the Second World War but was lovingly rebuilt and now lines up magnificently along the Elbe. In addition, Dresden is the gateway to the hiking paradise of Saxon Switzerland, where it's definitely worth taking a day trip.

How to get to Dresden

From Leipzig, you reach Dresden by train in 1h 35min and from Berlin in just under 2h. Since Dresden is so close to the Czech border, you are almost faster in Prague. The bus ride to the beautiful Czech capital takes just under 2 hours.

Dresden also has an international airport. The easiest and fastest way from the airport (DRS) to the main station is by S-Bahn. The journey takes about 20 minutes and costs 2.50 EUR.

Things to do in Dresden

Dresden has very beautiful buildings that invite you to explore them on a walk. If you don't visit a car museum in Stuttgart, you could visit the *VW Factory* here (Lennéstraße 1, 01069 Dresden). The visitor center is open Mon to Sat from 9 a.m. to 6.30 p.m. A guided tour lasts 45 minutes (every hour on the hour) and costs 9 EUR. You can also sign up for test drives.

A walking tour through Dresden

From the main train station, we walk towards **Kreuzkirche**, from where we continue to the beautiful **Frauenkirche**. This also looks beautiful at night when the middle cathedral is illuminated. The church was built in the 18th century in the Baroque style but was

destroyed in World War II. After the reunification of Germany, it was faithfully rebuilt and opened in 2005.

Nearby is the **Albertinum** Art Museum (Tue-Sun 10 a.m.—6 p.m., admission 12 EUR), where you can find works of art from the Romantic period to the present. By now the latest, you have to open your eyes well, because there are many pompous buildings in the area. Through the **Brühlsche Garten,** you come to the **Brühlsche Terrasse**, where you can rest on a bench with a good view or walk to the left along the Elbe. We walk up to **the Cathedral of Sanctissimae Trinitatis**. In this area, you find the magnificent **Semperoper** and the **Dresden Zwinger**. This dreamy building with many sculptures and a garden with ponds and fountains is really worth seeing. It also houses a museum with various exhibitions. Admission to the Gemäldegalerie Alte Meister, the Skulpturensammlung, the Mathematisch-Physikalischen Salon, and the Porzellansammlung costs 14 EUR (Tue-Sun 10 a.m. to 6 p.m.). The last stop on our city tour is the **Residenzschloss**. The castle served as the residence of the Saxon kings and electors and today houses several museums, including the **Green Vault**, which is one of the largest treasuries in Europe. The museums are open Tue-Sun from 10 a.m.-6 p.m. and admission only to the Green Vault is 14 EUR. In combination with the rest of the castle, the entrance fee is 24.50 EUR. So, if you want to visit several museums in Dresden, it is worth buying a *Dresden Museum Card* (25 EUR for two days).

Relax in the gardens

To relax in another green space within the city walk to the **Palais Großer Garten**. There you will find a pretty dahlia garden, ponds, fountains, and also the botanical garden. Admission is free and the greenhouses are open daily from 10 a.m.

A side trip for street art lovers

Another place worth seeing outside the old town is the **Kunsthofpassage**. For street art lovers, this neighborhood is a must. Each building in the Kunsthofpassage has its own theme and individual design inspired by nature, music, and imagination. Some of the remarkable buildings are the "Lichtspielhaus", which stands out for its impressive façade lighting, the "Regenhaus", which has become famous for its gutter music, and the "Courtyard of the Elements", which offers an experience for all the senses through its interaction with water and wind.

A trip to Saxon Switzerland

Although the landscape in the movie Avatar was inspired by a national park in China, the Elbe Sandstone Mountains in Saxon Switzerland also look quite similar. The main attraction is the **Bastei Bridge**, but you should definitely plan the time for a hike.

Every hour there is a train from Dresden to *Pirna*. There you change to bus 254 and get off at *Bastei, Lohmen*. The whole journey takes only 55 minutes. After you have enjoyed the view over the bridge, you could do the following great hike: Bus stop/parking Bastei - Schwedenlöcher - Amselgrund - Amselsee - Rathen - Basteibrücke - back to the starting point. This hike is just under 4 kilometers and takes about 1h 45 minutes.

Nuremberg

In addition to the world-famous Christmas market, Nuremberg trumps all year round with beautiful historic buildings scattered throughout the city center. For example, you can see the towers of the old city wall and countless impressive churches. If you still have time afterward, you can go shopping in Breite Gasse or the surrounding streets.

How to get to Nuremberg

Nuremberg has an international airport (NUE). The easiest and fastest way to get to the city center is by underground U2. Every 10 minutes it runs in the direction of the main station or vice versa and the journey takes 13 minutes.

From Munich, you are in Nuremberg by train in 1h, from Frankfurt or Leipzig in 2h, or from Ulm in 2h 30min. You can get to Rothenburg ob der Tauber in 1h 15min and to Bamberg in 35 minutes.

A city tour through Nuremberg

If you want to admire all the important sights, you can follow the succeeding route.

We start at the main station. If you have a heavy suitcase and do not stay overnight in Nuremberg, you should leave it in a locker now, because we will climb the castle hill later.

Just opposite the station is the **Frauentorturm**. Through the Frauentor you walk into a cute courtyard, with some restaurants and souvenir shops. The houses are designed as they used to look in medieval Nuremberg.

To your left, if you have time, you can look at art at the **Neues Museum Nuremberg** (www.nmn.de, Tue to Sun 10 a.m.- 6 p.m., 7 EUR, Sundays a visit to the collection is only 1 EUR). Otherwise, you stroll along the **Königstrasse**. Again, there is a wide selection of restaurants, ice cream parlors, and hotels. The first sight is the **St. Lawrence Church**, which suddenly towers in front of you.

Two minutes down the hill you reach the **museum bridge**, from which you have the perfect view of the beautiful

Heiligen-Geist-Spital restaurant. In the wine tavern, you could also enjoy a meal in this special building.

At **the Hauptmarkt**, you may be lucky that there is a market taking place and you can stroll through the stalls. Otherwise, the **Frauenkirche** is also an impressive building. In addition, you will find a richly decorated fountain (**Schöner Brunnen**) on the opposite side of the market square. There is a brass ring at the fountain. It is said that if you turn the ring and wish for something, the wish will come true.

Afterward, a short detour to the **Rathausplatz** is worthwhile.

We now follow the road up the hill to the **Kaiserburg**. Already when going up you should always take a look back because you have a nice view of some half-timbered houses and church towers. This field of vision widens a lot at the top of the castle terrace and you can also see more modern buildings in the distance. That's why the sweaty climb is worth every breath. In addition, you could have a drink upstairs in the café or treat yourself to a beer on the way. An inviting place for this is the square in front of **Albrecht Dürer's house**. We choose the route via Albrecht Dürer's House to get back down to the **Henkersbrücke**. No matter which alley you choose, you will marvel at many beautiful half-timbered houses. However, you will find particularly pretty examples along **Weißgerber Gasse**.

The Executioner's Bridge is, contrary to what you might expect because of the name, a very idyllic place. It is worth wandering around the bridges to capture all possible perspectives of this place. A little downstream you find the oldest suspension bridge in Germany. Do you dare to cross it?

Now we have arrived at the end of the ancient sights. With so much history, a guided city tour would of course also be a good idea. Free Walking Tours start daily at 11.30 a.m. at the fountain on the Main Market Square (www.nuremberg-freetour.com).

You can get back to the train station via the shopping district, where you should not miss the **Ehekarussell Brunnen** (fountain) by Hans Sachs.

Where to eat in Nuremberg

In addition to some bubble tea shops, Nuremberg surprised me with vegan sushi.

Vegan Vietnamese and Sushi

At first, I thought that there were probably spelling mistakes on the menu because there was vegan beef, vegan duck, and vegan salmon. In fact, all sushi and other food are prepared with vegan ingredients. I put together a whole tasting menu and everything was delicious! There should be more restaurants like this because I really wasn't missing meat or fish at all. You will find the restaurant **MY HAO** right next to the Museumsbrücke (König Straße 2) and despite the fabulous location, it is not expensive.

Where to stay in Nuremberg

If you like a lot of space in your hotel room, you should opt for the **Melter Hotel & Apartments** (https://melter.xyz/en). If you travel with children, it is convenient anyway to have a dining table and a small kitchen in the room. There even is a washing machine and dryer in the hotel, which you can use for free. The Wi-Fi worked perfectly and therefore, it is also well suited for business travelers. In addition, the bed was huge and extremely cozy and on the exquisite and comfortable deckchair, I could wonderfully relax my tired feet. The hotel is a four-minute walk from the train station and all the sights can be easily reached on foot.

Fairytale places that are also worth a visit

In Germany, there are many romantic cities that look as if they had sprung directly from a fairy tale. Of course, if you have enough time, you could spend half a day or a day in all these wonderful places. Maybe the charm of a trip to Germany lies in the decision that you would skip the big cities and visit the following treasures instead? If you want a good mix, you are spoilt for choice. You will be enchanted anyway, no matter which places you choose.

Bamberg

This pretty old town captivates visitors with the town hall, which is located in the middle of a bridge over the river Regnitz. The façade is richly painted with frescoes. The cathedral, which towers over the city, is also a UNESCO World Heritage Site and the climb up the hill is worthwhile.

How to get to Bamberg

From Nuremberg, you reach Bamberg by train in 40 minutes, from Erfurt in 45 minutes, and from Leipzig in 1h 30min.

A city tour in Bamberg

I had expected Bamberg to be a small village, which you can easily and quickly explore on foot. However, my calf muscles were quickly taught otherwise. From the main station it is a 20-minute walk to the old town and there the sights are spread over different hills. At least you can spare yourself the walk from the train station to the old town and take any bus that goes to the **ZOB**. The only attraction along the way is a futuristic bridge, which can also be seen from the bus. So, store your luggage at the luggage storage at the train station (from 2.50 EUR for 24 hours) and then let's go explore this beautiful, historic town.

One street away from the ZOB is a pretty **shopping street** and St. **Martin's Church.** Two minutes later you reach the famous bridge over the left arm of the Regnitz, where the beautiful **old town hall** stands. First, cross this bridge and then go to the left, where you cross the Regnitz again on the pretty **Geyersworthsteg**. Here you can get a different view of the town hall. Look around to see many more architecturally interesting **houses above the water**, which you can now visit up close. Or you can head to the **tourist information behind** a small **rose garden**.

Then you climb the hill to **Bamberg Cathedral**. Not to be confused with the Carmelite church on the hill to the left of the cathedral. In front of the cathedral, there is another **rose garden**, which is stunning, and above all, you have the best view over Bamberg from there. Then you choose a road that leads as straight as possible from the cathedral down to the river as there is an idyllic sight of the houses along the water. On Maps.me, the spot is marked as **"Ausblick auf Klein Venedig"** (View on Little Venice). You follow the river back to the

Ratshausbrücke and can now walk across the lower bridge. There you can even enjoy a delicious snack at tables on the bridge. Now we are done with the tour of the best sights in Bamberg and you could stroll back to the ZOB.

Quedlinburg

This historic town is best known for its medieval half-timbered architecture and baroque old town. Three churches characterize the place: the Marienkirche, the Schlosskirche, and the Nikolaikirche. Many old patrician houses, towers, and alleys line the streets of the old town. Here, too, the special Christmas market on the market square attracts numerous tourists every year.

Rothenburg ob der Tauber

Rothenburg ob der Tauber is a medieval town with numerous churches, museums, and beautiful half-timbered houses. A highlight of the city is the **Plönlein**, a passage under a clock tower that connects the old and new town hall. In addition, Rothenburg's

Christmas market is world-famous - with hot mulled wine and crispy gingerbread you can fully enjoy the magical charm of this small town.

By public transport, it was a bit cumbersome to get here. Therefore, first look for the best connection for you, so you can make sure that this trip fits into your itinerary. It would certainly be easier to reach this town by car.

Erfurt

The landmark of Erfurt is the **Krämerbrücke** and at the same time, it is one of the oldest bridges in Europe. It connects the eastern and western sides of the old town and consists of eleven houses in which shops are located. When crossing the bridge, you will be rewarded with a breathtaking view of the alleys and buildings of the historic city center. The Krämerbrücke is therefore not only architecturally remarkable but also conveys a feeling of timelessness and tradition.

Ulm

Ulm is an hour's train ride from Friedrichshafen and would even be feasible as a day trip from Switzerland. A visit to this extremely idyllic city is always worthwhile. Both in the fishing district and the shopping area, beautiful half-timbered houses are lined up. In addition, the Ulm Minster impresses with the highest church tower in the world.

Things to do in Ulm

Ulm is well manageable, and you can reach everything on foot. If you don't feel like exploring the sights anymore, you could also sit somewhere on the banks of the Danube or take a bike ride along the river.

Climb the Ulmer Münster

From anywhere in the city you can catch impressive views of this great cathedral. If you stand directly in front of it on the Münsterplatz, the historic building looks breathtaking. With 161.53m this is the highest church tower in the world, and you should therefore put Ulm on the tourist map just for this reason. For the daily workout, you can climb the tower via stairs. The highest of three viewing platforms is located at 143m. Until at least

summer 2024, however, the ascent will be renovated, and you can only get to the first platform at 70m. The entrance fee to the tower is currently 5 EUR. You can check this website (www.ulmer-muenster.de) to see if the top is accessible again.

Entry to the church is free and you should not miss the huge organ and the various artistic stained-glass windows. The tower is open from 9 a.m. to 5 p.m. (10 a.m. to 4 p.m. in winter) and masses take place on Sundays at 8.00 a.m., 9.30 a.m., and 6 p.m.

Walk through the fishermen's quarter

The idyllic *Fischer Viertel* is framed by the two narrow streams *Kleine Blau* and *Große Blau*. As a goal, you can set the Hotel *Schiefes Haus* on your map, which is one of the oldest houses in Ulm and even has an entry in the Guinness Book of Records as the most crooked hotel in the world. On the way to this venerable half-timbered house, you will see countless other great photo opportunities. It is probably the most idyllic neighborhood in Germany.

Hike the old city walls

The old red brick city wall is just behind the Hotel Schiefes Haus. The wall can only be reached by stairs. Further entrances with ramps can be found at *Wilhelmshöhe Park* and the *Herdbrücke*. From the wall, you can see more pretty half-timbered houses and you walk along the Danube.

Other interesting buildings and art

Back in the city center, you should definitely visit the town hall, whose façade is richly decorated. In addition, the **Museum Ulm** (https://museumulm.de/) is connected to the **Kunsthalle Weishaupt** (http://kunsthalle-weishaupt.de/) by a modern glass bridge. When we were there in the second last week of August, the museums had free admission for a whole week because of the school summer holidays.

The **Kunstverein Ulm** (https://kunstverein-ulm.de/, Kramgasse 4) always offers free temporary exhibitions (based on donations). During our visit, there just was a must-see exhibition of *Goin*, who makes similar stencil art as Banksy.

Where to eat in Ulm

With these many pretty half-timbered houses, all restaurants seem inviting. However, we found out that the Swabians like to make reservations and so we did not find a place in the Thai restaurant or Vietnamese restaurant near our hotel on Friday evening. Our rescue was the Asian takeaway in the station building. It also has food court-like tables and chairs, but it's not that cozy. However, the food was varied and super delicious, and the bubble tea was the cheapest I have drunk in Europe so far. It was good, too.

So if you have a restaurant favorite, you should make a reservation or otherwise, you have to expect to spend your evening with fast food.

Where to stay in Ulm

The **me and all hotel Ulm** (https://ulm.mean-dallhotels.com/) has a convenient location, directly opposite the main train station. You can therefore also retreat to the room during the day for a break, as you can reach all places in the city center from the hotel very quickly. Despite the proximity to the train station, it was absolutely quiet in the room and my daughter slept well in her sweetly furnished baby cot.

On the top floor, there is a stylish co-working area where you can also enjoy a delicious breakfast in the morning. All this with a view of the cathedral. You can treat yourself to delicious drinks in the *Über* Bar or relax on the great roof terrace. Speaking of drinks; everything in the minibar in the room is complimentary. The modern hotel rooms and the fitness room are designed in a poppy, but natural style. The *me and all hotel Ulm* definitely keeps up with the times and you will feel in good hands.

Munich

Munich is the second largest city in Germany. There are plenty of sights and good museums to discover, including Marienplatz, Frauenkirche, and Museum Brandhorst. The Deutsches Theater in Munich also offers a good program. In September, the city is packed, as Oktoberfest attracts party-loving people from all over the world. Even if there is no Oktoberfest, you should definitely try the delicious white sausages and pretzels in Munich. And of course, the various beers such as Paulaner, Augustiner, and Hacker Pschorr should not be missing. Before Christmas, there is a beautiful Christmas market on the market square and in the city center of Munich.

How to get from the airport to the city center

Often cheap flights fly to or from Munich (MUC) and there is a good chance that you will start or end your journey here. The cheapest way to transfer from the airport to the city center is the Lufthansa Express Bus (https://www.airportbus-muenchen.de/en). This bus runs every 20 minutes to the central station or vice versa and costs 11.50 EUR. The journey takes about 45 minutes.

The journey witl takes the same t 12.30 EUR.
A taxi would also take about 40 minutes and costs 70-80 EUR.

Things to do in Munich

Stroll through the Viktualien-markt, visit world-class art museums, relax in the English Garden, and enjoy the diverse gastronomic offer.

Taste yourself through the Viktualienmarkt

From Monday to Saturday, more than 250 retailers come to offer their products. The open-air market with covered market stalls is full of fresh fruit, vegetables, fish, and meat, as well as cheeses, bread, herbs, and spices from all over the world. A variety of tastes makes it a magnetic place for gourmets and connoisseurs. The stands are open from 8 a.m. to 8 p.m. Not all stands are open on Mondays. Near the market, you should not miss the beautiful Schrannenhalle. In this market hall, you will find small boutiques as well as traditional beer and wine bars.

Marvel at the most beautiful buildings in Munich

Start on Marienplatz at the beautiful **New Town Hall**. At 11, 12 and in summer also at 17 o'clock you can listen to the **carillon** and watch the colored figures moving on the façade.

The next stop is **Old Peter**, as the tower of St. Peter's Church is affectionately called. You can climb the tower for 5 EUR and thus gain a different view of the pretty buildings in Munich's old town. In clear weather, you can even see as far as the Alps. The tower is open daily from 9 a.m. to 6.30 p.m. Furthermore, the façade and the interior of the **Asam Church** are worth seeing. A walk past the magnificent **Palace of Justice** should not be missed and finally the beautiful **Residenz Munich**.

A short metro ride takes you to the Faculty of Mathematics of the Technical University of Munich. There is a worldwide unique **parabolic** slide (Boltzmannstraße 3) where you can slide down over three floors with a carpet. The slide can be used free of charge as long as the university is open. You simply need to do it quietly. Sliding is only recommended for people 11 years and older, as it is a pretty fast-paced run. Take a look at photos of the slide here: www.ma.tum.de/de/fakultaet/lage-anfahrt/bilder-parabelrutsche.html

A highlight at the end is the **Bavaria statue**. This statue towers over the Theresienwiese, where Oktoberfest and other events take place. What many do not know, however, is that you can climb a spiral staircase into the statue's head and enjoy the view through her eyes. The entrance fee is 5 EUR, and the platform is open daily from April to October from 9 a.m. to 6 p.m.

Stroll through Munich's diverse gardens

The **English Garden** is one of the largest urban parks in the world and offers visitors a wealth of recreational opportunities. In summer you can walk, ride and relax on the beaches. In winter there are ice rinks, bobsleigh lifts, and cross-country ski slopes. There also are many pubs, cafes, and restaurants in the park.

The largest beer garden in the world is in the **Hirschgarten** and if you would like to enjoy a beer or a small meal outdoors you are exactly in the right spot there.

In the **Olympic Garden,** you walk past many sculptures and there is also an amphitheater, a water fountain, many cozy benches, and avenues that are shaded by trees.

The beautiful garden of **Nymphenburg Palace** is accessible free of charge. Here alone you could spend half a day to a day in summer and enjoy the many sculptures, fountains, and lakes or treat yourself to a gondola ride on the canal. The fountains are bubbling from Easter to mid-October daily from 10 a.m. to 12 noon and from 2 p.m. to 4 p.m. I was also there in winter and with snow, it still looked very fairytale-like, even if the water attractions were not in operation.

Watch surf experts in the river or dare to ride the wave yourself

At the southern end of the English Garden, you find the Eisbachwelle (Prinzregenten-straße), where surfers venture into the cool water with their boards. On warm days, the spectacle attracts both surfers and spectators.

Go shopping

Munich has many beautiful shopping streets, where you can linger at well-known brand stores and in local boutiques. Especially the area between Karlsplatz (Stachus) and Marienplatz makes the hearts of shopping queens and kings beat faster.

Admire the masterpieces in a museum

Munich has some really great museums and on Sundays, they often cost only 1 EUR. If you are interested in art, you should definitely see the unique masterpieces of the **Alte Pinakothek** and the **Pinakothek der Moderne** (www.pinakothek.de). **Museum Brandhorst** houses Europe's largest collection of paintings by Andy Warhol (www.museum-brandhorst.de).

In the **Lenbachhaus** (www.lenbachhaus.de), which is known for its large collection of paintings by the group Blauer Reiter and Franz Marc, visitors can enter the exhibition free of charge every 1st Thursday of the month from 6 p.m. to 10 p.m. In the **Haus der Kunst** (www.hausderkunst.de/) the "Open Haus" takes place on the last Friday of the month between 4 and 10 p.m. Every Tuesday only half the admission is charged at the Kunsthalle München (www.kunsthallemuc.de/).

Where to eat or drink in Munich

The **Augustiner Keller** is a brewery pub with delicious dishes and beer in the traditional Bavarian style. The **Hofbräuhaus** is one of the most visited restaurants in the world and still convinces today with the typical Bavarian drinks and food. **Bahnwärter Thiel** is a colorful outdoor club where you can enjoy good drinks in a relaxed atmosphere. If you need something sweet after that, **Wir machen Cupcakes** offers pretty and delicious cupcakes and other patisseries.

Neuschwanstein Castle

Neuschwanstein Castle is an enchanting fairytale castle located in Schwangau near Füssen in the Allgäu. It was built at the request of King Ludwig II of Bavaria. Its distinctive architecture has even inspired the Disney Castle and the similarities are easy to see. For all people with a romantic streak or all wannabe princesses, a trip to the Allgäu is definitely worth taking!

How to get to Neuschwanstein Castle

Neuschwanstein Castle is located in Hohenschwangau near Füssen, 220 km from Stuttgart and 120 km from Munich. With a rental car, you can easily do the trip from either of the two cities. Parking costs 8 EUR and is located 1.5 km from the castle. The walk uphill takes about 40 minutes. However, you can take a shuttle bus (round trip 3 EUR) or take a horse-drawn carriage (uphill 7 EUR, downhill 3.50 EUR).

If you don't have a rental car, you can book a group day trip from Munich (ask locally for current offers) or you can take the train:

First, you ride from Munich to **Füssen** (there are hourly connections). There you only have a short transfer time to get on **bus 78** to Neuschwanstein Castle. The total journey time takes about 2h30 and starts at 24 EUR without other discounts.

What you can expect from a guided tour at the castle

The tour lasts about 30 minutes and costs 15 EUR if you buy the tickets at the ticket center in Hohenschwangau. Careful, it may well be that all tours are already fully booked on that day, or you have to wait up to 3 hours for the next tour. Therefore, it is better if you buy the tickets in advance in the online shop (17.50 EUR, https://shop.ticket-center-hohenschwangau.de/).

The tour begins with a conversation about the life and vision

of King Ludwig II. Quickly, the romance that surrounded the castle begins to crumble, as you realize that the whole royal family was a bit crazy.

You will also learn more about the architecture of the castle and the influence of the medieval style elements. On the tour, you will be guided through several rooms where original furniture and works of art are located. After visiting the throne room, you also have the opportunity to enjoy the impressive view from the castle tower or the surrounding mountain landscape.

In addition to the guided tour

Neuschwanstein Castle is especially worth seeing from the outside. Therefore, in good weather, you should definitely continue to the **Marienbrücke** (15 minutes from the castle), from where you have the best location for a photo. In case of snow or slippery tracks, however, this path is closed.

You could also visit the yellow **Hohenschwangau Castle** if you haven't seen enough royal décor up close (21 EUR).

Beautiful places on Lake Constance

Lake Constance is surrounded by Germany, Austria, and Switzerland. From the idyllic shores, you have a view of the Alps, and the pretty towns invite you for a stroll. Following, I mention some of the most beautiful places on the western shore of Lake Constance. Of course, a jump into the water is also a nice activity everywhere or you can take a bike ride on the Lake Constance cycle path.

Meersburg

Meersburg is one of the most idyllic towns on Lake Constance. The city is known for its beautiful medieval architecture. Walkers on the cobblestone streets get an insight into the rich cultural history and also the cyclists who are on the Lake Constance bicycle path like to get off their bikes here to enjoy the charm of Meersburg.

If you have enough energy to explore the hilly countryside, **Meersburg Castle** offers visitors the chance to admire medieval architecture and learn more about its history. In the castle, there is also a museum (daily from 10 a.m. to 6.30 p.m. (until 6 p.m. in winter), 12.80 EUR) with interesting exhibits from the 12th century. In addition, the location offers a breathtaking view of the lake.

Apart from the old castle, Meersburg is also home to the **New Castle**.

Otherwise, there are several wineries around Meersburg, in whose wine cellars you can taste their products.

Constance

Constance attracts tourists from near and far who stroll through the beautiful old town. There are many stores where you can shop to your heart's desire, both in the old town and in the Lago shopping center. There is a wide selection of good restaurants and cafés. My favorite cafes were

Das Vogelhaus and the *Pano*. Both cafes are still great, but unfortunately, they have become such popular meeting places that there is always a high-volume level and sometimes you don't

get a seat. Nevertheless, you could try your luck.

In the old town, you should visit the **Kaiserbrunnen** and the **Konstanzer Münster**.

From the port in Constance, you can take ship tours on Lake Constance or take a trip to the island of **Mainau** (see next chapter). In addition, the harbor park invites you to stroll along the water. The **Imperia statue** at the harbor was created by Peter Lenk as a tribute to the writer and poet Victor Hugo, who wrote a love story during the Council of Constance in the 15th century. The statue is also an allusion to the corruption and moral decay that took place during the Council of Constance. The two little men held by the woman are said to represent the powerful and influential of the time, who profited from prostitution and other immoral activities.

The **Bodensee-Therme Konstanz,** which can be reached by bus in 25 minutes from the Konstanz train station, has many fantastic saunas. It also has indoor and outdoor hot pools and you can jump into the lake both in summer and winter. 3,5h sauna, thermal bath, and outdoor pool cost 24.50 EUR.

From the Konstanz train station you can walk along Lake Constance (to the right) to Kreuzlingen in Switzerland.

Mainau – The Flower Island

This island is connected to the land by a bridge. You cannot enter the island for free, as there are beautiful gardens all over the island, which cost admission. The gardens are open daily from 9 a.m. to 5 p.m. Of course, the visit is especially worthwhile when the flowers are blooming, so the entrance fee in summer is higher. In winter prices start at 10.50 EUR and in summer from 24.50 EUR with the online ticket (www.mainau.de/de/informationen-service.html).

By bus, you can reach the island of Mainau from Constance in 35 minutes. You can check the current boat schedule and possible combined tickets for trip and admission on this website (www.bsb.de).

Black Forest

The Black Forest is known for good wellness hotels, cuckoo clocks, and beautiful landscapes. This landscape can be wonderfully explored on a road trip. On the other hand, we always lose a lot of time in the Black Forest when driving over all these hills and with the many construction sites. So, if you don't like driving, you should stay in one place and let yourself get pampered at the hotel or explore the local sights. From a culinary point of view, you have to treat yourself to a piece of original Black Forest cake (Schwarzwälder Torte).

Some places can be reached by train, others by bus, but the easiest way is if you have your own vehicle.

Sights in the Black Forest

I will describe the Black Forest treetop path in the chapter of Karlsruhe. However, I would rather advise you against its visit. However, you should not miss the following places.

Triberg

The cute but very touristy village of Triberg is located at the foot of the Black Forest. The houses in the center are all built in the typical Black Forest architecture and give the village its special charm. From here, visitors can then set off on hikes in the beautiful landscape of the Black Forest, for example to the nearby **Triberg waterfalls**. They are the highest waterfalls in Germany. We were there in the summer and were a bit disappointed as not much water flowed and the water falls over several steps (so, it's not one giant fall). Per-

haps a visit after the snow melts in spring is better. In addition, it is a long way from the lower parking lot to the waterfall and a very steep path from the upper parking lot. The descent is at least 200 meters and after that, you follow the waterfall (163m) down as well (and in the end back up). You must therefore allow at least two hours for the waterfall visit. The entrance fee to the waterfall is 8 EUR.

House of 1000 Clocks

This is a souvenir shop, which can be found in several places in the Black Forest. The shops are beautifully designed and the many elaborately created cuckoo clocks are absolutely worth seeing. So you shouldn't think of the House of 1000 Clocks as a shop, but as a free museum.

Titisee

The Titisee is a beautiful mountain lake in the heart of the Black Forest, which invites you to hike, swim, and ride pedalo boats.

Feldberg

At 1493 meters, the Feldberg is the highest mountain in the Black Forest and a popular ski resort in winter.

Black Forest Open-Air Museum Vogtsbauernhof

This open-air museum shows life and work in the Black Forest in past centuries. It is a popular destination for those interested in culture. It is open daily from 9 a.m. to 6 p.m. from the end of March to the beginning of November. The entrance fee for adults is 12,00 €. With the SchwarzwaldCard the visit is free.

Hohenzollern Castle

The beautiful castle looks a bit like Hogwarts from the outside. It is the ancestral seat of the Princes of Hohenzollern and the Prussian royal family. The entrance fee is 22.00 EUR

and the royal interior is very impressive. You can reach the castle by taking the train to *Hechingen* and changing to a bus there.

From the car park, it would be a well-signposted 25-minute walk to the castle or you use the shuttle bus.

Baden Baden

This city is all about thermal springs, beauty, and luxury. Thus, for example, famous horse races take place here every year and you can spend your money in the casino. Even without money, Baden Baden is attractive, because the beautiful flower gardens and the good view from the castle can be visited for free.

How to get to the city center from the train station

The fact that the rich and famous prefer to come to Baden Baden in expensive cars is also shown because the train station is located 10 driving minutes outside the city center. This is not a problem in itself, as there are bus connections to the center every 15 minutes, but you just have to plan more time when you leave or arrive by train.

Things to do in Baden Baden

The obvious thing would be to relax in a thermal bath. However, you can also have fun outside the water in Baden Baden.

Stroll through the gardens

Baden Baden would be a good place for a health retreat because you can walk almost endlessly through beautiful public gardens. The 20-minute walk from the city center to Lichtenthal Monastery is especially nice. The avenue consists of beautiful, shady trees and on the way, you can stop at the Gönneranlage, where there are many roses and then a little further you find fantastic dahlia blossoms.

If you still haven't had enough of fairytale flowers, you can pay a visit to the *Rosenneuheiten Garten* on the Beutig (Moltkestraße 3, 76530 Baden-Baden). There you can see award-winning rose plants and some statues. The entrance fee is 1 EUR. The garden is only open from May to October. By car you, unfortunately, have to take quite a detour until you arrive at the garden and also by bus (e.g., bus 216 to stop Stadelhoferstraße) you have to walk at least 8 minutes. Nevertheless, this beautiful garden is worth a visit.

Walk to the New Castle (Neues Schloss)

The New Castle towers high above Baden Baden and the journey is the destination. Find a path through the pretty alleys in Baden Baden and let yourself be enchanted by the cute town. The more altitude you gain, the better your view of the place will be.

Visit the most important buildings

In Baden Baden, there are several buildings worth seeing with richly decorated facades. The first remarkable building you see from the bus when you come from the train station is the Festspielhaus.
Afterward, you should take a look at the pump room in the beautiful park on Kaiserallee. You can walk in the Wandelhalle and look at the murals. Right next to it is the lovely casino and the tourist information, which is located in a small outdoor mall along with other shops.

Relax in a spa

After all, you come to this spa town for a bath. The thermal springs were discovered by the Romans 2000 years ago when the first baths were built. A modern answer to this is the *Caracalla Therme*. Two hours of sauna and bath cost 24 EUR (opening hours: daily from 8 a.m. to 10 p.m.). Ancient architecture can be found in the *Friedrichsbad*. The choice of water pools and saunas (only a steam sauna) is more limited, but the rooms are more historic, and slippers, towels, tea, shampoo, and body lotion are included in the entrance fee (35 EUR).

Where to stay in Baden Baden

In the hotel **Der Kleine Prinz** (www.derkleineprinz.de/en/) you can enjoy a fairytale interior design. Especially in the breakfast room, you feel like in a castle, but also the courtyard of the restaurant is very inviting. There is a lounge with comfortable sofas and a pool table, and throughout the house, you can find paintings from the story of the Little Prince by Antoine de Saint-Exupéry. Also, my suite was royally furnished, with high-quality, antique décor and yet modern comfort. It even had a bubble function in the big bathtub and the bed was huge.

If you are looking for an exquisite garden in addition to the beautiful rooms, where you can rest in deckchairs, you should stay at the sister hotel **Belle Epoque** (www.hotel-belle-epoque.de/en/). As the name suggests, the beautifully designed hotel fits perfectly into pretty Baden Baden.

Stuttgart

Stuttgart is the sixth largest city in Germany and is located in the southwest of the country. The city is home to two automobile museums of world-famous brands. The Schlossplatz, the Königsstraße, the Staatsgalerie, the Rosensteinpark, and the market square also invite you to do a city tour. Moreover, Stuttgart offers a variety of shopping facilities and gastronomic delights for every taste.

How to get from the airport to the city center

From Stuttgart Airport (STR) you can easily reach the city center by S-Bahn. The journey takes 30 minutes and costs 3.40 EUR.

Things to do in Stuttgart

Whether shopping or museums, there is a lot to see in Stuttgart.

Visit the automobile museums

You can choose between Porsche and Mercedes Benz. I liked both museums and they are already worth seeing because of the architecture of the buildings. So either you visit both museums or choose the car brand you like better. In the end, I liked the

Mercedes Museum (Mercedesstraße 100, Tue-Sun 9 a.m. – 6 p.m., 12 EUR, evening ticket from 4.30 p.m. 6 EUR) a little bit better, because the tour starts with a futuristic elevator ride and the exhibition deals with various topics, about history, art, and culture and what happened while the brand developed into today's state.

More information about the Porsche Museum (S-Bahn stop "Neuwirtshaus/Porscheplatz", Tue-Sun 9 a.m.-6 p.m., 10 EUR) can be found on the website: www.porsche.com/germany/aboutporsche/porschemuseum/openinghoursandprices/.

Admire art in the Staatsgalerie

The State Gallery is huge and many famous paintings are hanging in the exhibition. Just to visit all the rooms without really being able to pay attention to every picture took me two hours. Therefore, plan enough time for this museum (www.staatsgalerie.de/besuch/besuchplanen.html, Tue-Sun 10 a.m. - 5 p.m., Thu until 8 p.m., 7 EUR, every Wed the collection is free).

Visit the library

The library in Stuttgart (Mailänder Platz 1) is worth seeing not only because of the books but also because of the spacious, minimalist architecture. In addition, there is a free terrace on the roof, from which you can enjoy a view over Stuttgart.

Other places to visit in the city

The Schlossplatz is a large public square in the center of Stuttgart and an important meeting place for locals and tourists alike. The square is surrounded by several historic buildings, including the New Castle, the Old Castle, and the Collegiate Church. In addition, the Schlossplatz is an important venue for celebrations.

Another beautiful place outdoors is the **Rosensteinpark**. It is a pretty park known for its scenic walks, ponds, and gardens. It offers numerous leisure facilities such as tennis courts, a playground, and a beer garden.

If you've had enough of nature, you can head to **Königsstraße**, Stuttgart's most important shopping street and one of the busiest pedestrian zones in Germany. It stretches over a length of about 1.2 kilometers and offers numerous shops, restaurants, and cafés.

Karlsruhe

I didn't have this city on my radar at first, because Karlsruhe is unfortunately not as present on blogs as other German cities on the tourist trail. However, at least a stopover is absolutely worthwhile because here you will find several pretty castles and a huge, green oasis of relaxation within walking distance.

What to do in Karlsruhe

If you have limited time, a two-hour stop is enough to see the sights in the city center and to grab a snack. Since especially in summer many activities are offered, such as an open-air cinema, you can also spend a few nights in Karlsruhe and visit the sights in the suburbs or make a day trip to the Black Forest.

Visit the castles in Karlsruhe

The main attraction is the beautiful **Karlsruhe Palace**, which is 2.5 km from the main train station. If you don't want to walk, take a tram in the direction of the market square. The outer castle area is accessible free of charge, and you fill your camera with amazing pictures. Nowadays, the castle houses the **Badisches Landesmuseum**. It is closed on Mondays, otherwise open from 10-5 p.m. (Tue-Thu) and 10-6 p.m. (Fri-Sun). The entrance fee is 8 EUR from 17 years and older. On Fridays from 2 p.m., however, it is free of charge and at 4 p.m. there is a free guided tour of the castle.

Another building worth seeing is **Gottesaue Castle**. It has a salmon-colored façade and cute turrets. 5 minutes within walking distance, at the tram station *Wolfartsweierer Straße*, you will also find a good sushi restaurant (*Sushi Park*).

Recharge your batteries in the gardens

If you look at the map of Karlsruhe, you will see several large green areas. One of them is the pretty palace garden behind Karlsruhe Palace. If you don't just want to walk, bike, or lie down on the grass, there also is a small tourist train and a pond with water lilies and ducks.

The botanical garden with various species of flowers borders the castle garden. The public areas are accessible free of charge, but access to the greenhouses costs 3 EUR.

Stroll through the bustling center of Karlsruhe

The most beautiful passage of the shopping street is located between Marktplatz and Europaplatz. There you will find all sorts of shops and international restaurants. If you are at the candy-colored town hall on the market square at the top of the hour, you can listen to the carillon, which plays whole songs. There also is a pyramid as a nice photo opportunity.

If you have space in your luggage and are still looking for furnishings, there is also an Ikea and a huge XXXLutz at the tram station *Weinweg*. For us, this was very convenient, as we had just moved into a new apartment and these furniture stores were right on the way to our hotel.

Ride the oldest funicular in Germany

If you are in Karlsruhe for more than half a day, you should also visit the district of Durlach, which you can easily reach in 10 minutes by tram. There you can look at medieval half-timbered houses in the center and a beautiful fountain with animal figures at the Karlsburg. Durlach is also home to Germany's oldest funicular. With it, you can ride up the *Turmberg*. It costs 3

EUR each way. However, you can also reach the viewing terrace on foot (the locals use the ascent as a workout) or by bus/car. However, I did not find the view over the city and the many industrial chimneys so spectacular and therefore I only recommend this detour if you are interested in the funicular.

Treat yourself to a delicious Asian meal

Karlsruhe has many Asian restaurants. We had a delicious meal at *Tawa Yama* in Karlsruhe-Durlach. It is an Asian fusion restaurant, which also offers extremely delicious vegetarian dishes, that are also nicely presented. Since it is located in an industrial area (7 minutes' walk from the tram station Durlach Auer Straße) the prices are comparatively cheap for such an upscale cuisine. Try the tempura cauliflower or the matcha ice cream.

Delicious bubble tea can be found next to the Hans im Glück burger restaurant on Europaplatz (inside the building).

Where to stay in Karlsruhe

We had two very good nights at **Hotel Der Blaue Reiter** (https://hotelderblaureiter.de/en/).

This stylish hotel, which is richly decorated with art, has made a name for itself as a seminar hotel. However, I also felt really comfortable during my tourist stay. The staff at the reception was very friendly and our spacious, modern suite had a bathtub with a bubble function. The bed was huge and extremely comfortable and thanks to the good air conditioning we slept wonderfully even in these midsummer temperatures. Even for our toddler, they have lovingly provided some useful everyday objects in the room. The breakfast buffet was varied and tasty. Within walking distance of the hotel there are some pretty half-timbered houses in the historic center of Karlsruhe-Durlach. Plus, you can reach the delicious Asian fusion restaurant Tawa Yama, as well as some ice cream parlors on foot. In 10 minutes, you can get to the castle in Karlsruhe by tram.

Take a day trip to the Black Forest Treetop Walk

From Karlsruhe, you reach Bad Wildbad in 1h by train (40 minutes by car), where the Black Forest Treetop Walk is located. It is a beautiful treetop path with a great tower at the end and you can enjoy magnificent views over the vast Black Forest all the time. After that, however, the positive points end.

The excursion is quite expensive, as access to the path costs 11.50 EUR. If you want to go down the slide at the end (which of course you do since you are there anyway), you pay 2 EUR extra. Below the treetop path is a large, fenced forest playground, which costs a 7 EUR entrance fee per person (even for the parents). If you walk another 15 minutes, you will come to a suspension bridge that belongs to another company and costs 9 EUR if you want to cross it. In addition, the treetop path is located secluded on a mountain. After you have spent the fuel for the steep ride, you also pay the 3 EUR parking fee per 2h or you go up with the summer cable car (round trip 7 EUR per person), with the modern funicular. Sure, the tower from the treetop path has an architectural appeal and the view is fantastic. However, there is the same construction of the treetop path (at the bottom of the website: www.baum-wipfelpfade.de/schwarz-wald/) in 10 other places in Europe and maybe one of them is more accessible for you.

Heidelberg

Heidelberg is considered one of the most beautiful and historic cities in Germany. It's best to simply go on an extensive city tour so that you don't miss any of the magnificent buildings.

The beautiful **Heidelberg Castle** towers over the city in all its glory. Also, the pretty University of **Heidelberg** should not be missed. It houses the world's largest university library with over 4 million books. Other sights include the **Alte Brücke** over the Neckar, the **Alte Bau,** and the **Church of the Holy Spirit**. In addition, the city center of Heidelberg is full of charming wine bars, boutiques, and historical monuments.

Mannheim

Mannheim attracts travelers because of its vibrant cultural life and picturesque old town. The parks are also impressive. For example, **the Luisenpark** with its impressive lake landscapes and botanical gardens. In the **castle garden,** you can take a leisurely walk or jog and discover the graceful buildings that surround the garden. Finally, there is the **rose garden**. With the characteristic water tower, this garden is a must! As it is a university town, it is also teeming with good bars and restaurants. In summer, a visit to the **Neckar beach** (www.neckarstrand-mannheim.de) is worthwhile. Here you can enjoy a glass of wine or beer at sunset, sip on your cocktails, and relax with live music.

Frankfurt am Main

In the past, I had only made it to the airport in Frankfurt, which is a huge hub in Europe. Now I could finally visit the city, which is a mixture of the old town with venerable

churches and shiny financial skyscrapers.

My first impression when I walked out of the train station building, however, was a shock. The square in front of the station is teeming with drug addicts and, unfortunately, the smell of urine reaches far into the Kaiserstraße. In the hotel, I was told that this has lamentably been the case for a long time and that it is better to avoid this region in the evening. Too bad, because there are a lot of restaurants along this street. At the shopping malls, along the river, and in the historic center, however, it's a much better picture, and therefore, you should still give Frankfurt a chance.

How to get to Frankfurt

Almost every traveler passes by the bustling Frankfurt Airport (FRA) at some point. The city center is easily and quickly accessible by S-Bahn. The journey takes 15 minutes and costs 5.20 EUR.

From Cologne, you reach Frankfurt in 1 to 2 hours by train (look for the best connection), from Mannheim in 36 minutes, from Heidelberg in 1h to 1h 30min, and from Stuttgart in 1h 30min.

Things to do in Frankfurt

You can spend a day in Mainhatten in many ways. Here are some ideas.

Along and on the river Main

The Main definitely gives the skyline of Frankfurt an extra sparkle. In some places, people dangle their feet in the water in the summer and you can also rent canoes or stand-up boards. To get a good overview of all the interesting bridges, while a tape informs you about the city sights, you should take a city tour with a boat of the *KD line*. That way you have a good overview of Frankfurt right at the beginning. The 60-minute trip starts at the bridge "Eiserner Steg" (where tickets can be bought in a kiosk at the water) and

goes upstream to the locks and downstream to the Westhafen. The trip costs only 12 EUR, which is cheaper and more efficient than the neighbors of the *Primus line*, which does the same program in 100 minutes with a stop in the middle back at the ticket house. There, you can pay 12 EUR for the 50-minute trip but will only see one side of the river. From the boat, you have a great view of Frankfurt and can enjoy the sight from the comfort of a chair.

If you want to burn some calories, you can take a walk along the Main. The shoreside does not matter, because there are good paths for jogging or cycling on both sides (e.g. Mainkai).

Visit the half-timbered houses and churches on the Römerbergplatz

This is the center of the old town and a truly great photo subject. Also worth seeing are the cathedral and the town hall. The *Schirn Kunsthalle* is modern, yet harmonious with its surroundings. Check the website (www.schirn.de) to see which exhibition is currently on site (closed on Mondays.)

Visit a museum

In addition to the Schirn Kunsthalle, another good art museum is the Städel Museum. It is located across the river on the Museumsufer. In addition, there are several small free galleries on Kaiserstraße near Willy-Brandt-Platz.

For children, the Senckenberg Museum (https://museumfrankfurt.sensenckenb.de/de/besuch) is a good choice. Already on the forecourt, you can see two life-size dinosaur figures.

Take a walk in a garden

If you are looking for an oasis of greenery, you have several options in Frankfurt. For example, there is the Chinese Garden in **Bethmannpark**, which has been laid out according to the principles of Feng Shui. In addition to Asian-looking wooden pavilions, there also is a pond.

Secondly, of course, the **botanical garden** is inviting with many spice plants at *Grüneburgpark*. It is open from March to October and accessible free of charge, as is the small **Korean garden** next door.

The large **palm garden** has a 7 EUR entrance fee, where you can look at beautiful palm greenhouses and a butterfly building or paddle around on the lake with pedalo boats or play mini golf. Additionally, there is a great water playground. The palm garden is also open in winter.

Watch a performance at the Alte Oper

The Alte Oper is a very beautiful building and therefore worth seeing from the outside. Although it is called old opera, Broadway musicals are often performed. In August, a great adventure playground for children was set up on the square in front of the opera. For example, the children could paddle around the fountain in small boats. What a funny idea! Maybe another event is taking place on the forecourt during your visit. Have a look.

Treat yourself to a Frankfurt apple wine

The *Ebbelwei* is a specialty from here and must of course be tried. This refreshing wine made from alcoholized apples is best drunk with a Franconian meal in Frankfurt's nightlife district, Sachsenhausen. The center of the action with really pretty pubs and benches in courtyards is on *Klappergasse*. *Mrs. Rauscher* also has a fountain figure, which spits at regular intervals on the passers-by. I am almost surprised that this fountain is not yet as famous as Manneken Pis in Belgium.

Where to stay in Frankfurt

The **AMERON Frankfurt Neckarvillen Boutique** (https://ameroncollection.com/de/frankfurt-neckarvillen-boutique) convinces with a stylish interior design and many art elements. In the lobby, there is a nice salon for drinking coffee and doing some work. As a

welcome, there were delicious, homemade chocolates in the room and also at the reception, there was always fruit-enriched water and delicious snacks. The hotel kitchen is therefore recommended for breakfast as well as for lunch and dinner in the restaurant *Le Petit Royal Frankfurt*. The boutique hotel has a very nice wellness area with sun beds and a Finnish sauna. Right next to it is a well-equipped gym. Both can be used exclusively free of charge upon reservation. You can relax in the Neckarvillen Boutique after sightseeing or after a visit to the famous trade fair and feel in good hands. In these midsummer temperatures, I was happy about the good air conditioning in the room. At the same time, however, there also was a pleasant underfloor heating in the bathroom. I would love to come back to this nice hotel.

Where to eat in Frankfurt

Le Petit Royal Frankfurt, which is located in the AMERON Frankfurt Neckarvillen boutique, offers first-class meat and fish dishes and vegetarians will also have their mouths watering. We tried our way through the menu and were especially enthusiastic about the tartar and the caviar. The main course was a juicy steak with crispy homemade French fries, a tender fish fillet with beans, and a delicious truffle risotto. The portions are very generous so that even hungry men will be full. Luckily, we still had a bit of space for the in-house chocolates and the refreshing mango sorbet for dessert. Just because of these delicious chocolates, I would return to *Le Petit Royal Frankfurt* or the Neckarvillen boutique.

By the way, this is also one of the few restaurants in Europe where you can treat yourself to original Kobe beef. Enjoy your meal!

Düsseldorf

In this city along the Rhine, I especially noticed the friendly inhabitants. For example, drivers always stopped and let me cross the road, which is, unfortunately, less and less the case in Switzerland. Therefore, I can already recommend Düsseldorf if you need a more positive light on your own view of the world. Apart from that, Düsseldorf attracts visitors with countless good restaurants and shops. There even is a Little Tokyo with many Asian restaurants and shops, but vegetarians and vegans also have plenty of options. The sights themselves you'll have ticked off quickly, but afterward, the restaurants, the longest bar in the world, and the Düsseldorf Altbier, which leads a tough competition with the Kölsch from Cologne, require your attention. The feud between the two cities is so big that German friends of mine, who lived in Cologne for 6 years, had never even visited Düsseldorf in the whole time (the cities are 25 minutes apart). As a tourist, fortunately, you do not have to worry about such things and can well visit both cities, because it is definitely worth it.

From the airport to the city center

DUS Airport is another major hub in Europe and it may well be that the cheapest flight ticket to Germany will land you here. In 30 minutes you reach the center with the S11 for 6.10 EUR.

Things to do in Düsseldorf

If you didn't just come to eat or shop, you should check out the following sights.

Stroll along the Rhine promenade

Düsseldorf is strongly connected to the Rhine and you can enjoy the river on a walk along the promenade that is several kilometers long. If you don't just want to go for a walk, you can eat or drink something near the *Düsseldorf water level clock* in inviting outdoor pubs directly on the water.

Explore the Media Harbor

This is a modern district whose buildings make the hearts of architects or photographers beat faster. You should start with the curved and shiny **Gehry buildings** (Neuer Zollhof) and then follow the water across the bridge to the Hyatt Regency. Various buses and trams go back to the city center, or you walk along the Rhine promenade, which is a must anyway if you haven't come this way yet.

Take the lift to the top of the Rhine Tower

Although it feels like every city in Germany has a television tower on which you can enjoy the view, the Rhine Tower in Düsseldorf (www.rheinturm.de) is very worthwhile. The Rhine bends at the foot of the tower and you have a beautiful view over the bridges and the city. The Media Harbor is also located directly under the tower, which allows you to enjoy the great architecture of the buildings from a new perspective. For 10 EUR you get to the bar M168 with the elevator in a few seconds, where you can enjoy the 360-degree panoramic view. In the first and last hour of the day, the lift ride costs only 6 EUR.

Sunbathe on Paradise Beach

Under the Rhine Tower is the Rheinpark. Take the pedestrian bridge *Parlamentufer*, from which you have another good view of the Media Harbor. On the other side, you can already see the sandy beaches along the Rhine. I was here on a foggy October day and therefore there was not much with swimming, but in the summer, people bathe there, as far as I know. Just remember that it's a river and it could still have unexpected currents.

Visit the sights of the Old Town

You can start at the **Radschlä-gerbrunnen** at the Maritime Museum. In general, you should pay attention in Düsseldorf, where you see figures or sculptures that are doing a cartwheel. Door handles, shaft covers, and chocolate bars are covered with such decorations. The origin of this tradition is not entirely clear, but even today children enjoy being able to take part in cartwheel competitions.

Then you make a short detour to the **town hall**, where you turn into Bolkerstraße. Here you find the **longest open-air counter in the world**. Seat after seat of various bars and restaurants is lined up. Also worth seeing is the cute **Schneider-Wibbel-Gasse**. Look for the wall decoration at the entrance of the alley, which gives wise advice about money. Afterward, you could pay a visit to the **Düsseldorf mustard shop** and take a look at the **Old Harbor**. Now you are probably hungry again and can fill your stomach at the covered **market stalls on Carlsplatz**. There is everything from Munich brewery food to Indian samosas.

Stroll along the Kö

In Dusseldorf, it is extremely difficult not to start a shopping spree. The reason for this is the Königsallee, called "Kö", which runs along the riverbed. On both sides, there are well-known clothing shops and department stores. In the *Schadow-Arkaden* there is also a food court in the basement if you haven't yet got stuck somewhere in an ice cream parlor or a restaurant. Don't miss the *Kö-Bogen*. Even if you don't want to shop, this building next to the park with the Northern Düssel is an interesting photo subject.

Little Tokyo

Let's get back to feasting. Düsseldorf also has a close connection to Japanese culture and celebrates **Japan Day in mid-May**. In addition, the Little Tokyo district is located near the station. Apart from Japanese restaurants, you will also find Asian shops and many Korean restaurants.

Again, you should better reserve for the evening. I spontaneously didn't get a single seat on a Sunday.

If you prefer to eat local food, you can try the *HeimWerk* or Restaurant *Zum Schiffchen* near the old port.

Kiefernstraße Graffiti

Along Kiefernstraße, all building facades are painted with colored murals. These paintings are worth seeing and the history of the houses is unusual. Actually, this neighborhood should have been re-planned in the 1980s, which would have led to housing shortages among the residents. Therefore, the apartments were illegally occupied until a solution was found with the city.

If you walk from the Media Harbor to here and visit the old town and Kö in between, you will cover about 10 km. It's doable, but maybe it would be more practical, with a rented bike or you treat yourself to a ride on public transport (3 EUR for each ride or a day ticket, which gets cheaper the bigger your group is).

A trip to Tiger & Turtle – Magic Mountain

This walk-in roller coaster sculpture has been in Duisburg since 2011 and still has not lost its appeal. Another reason to visit this sculpture is that the entrance to the construction is completely free. When the many LED lamps glow in the dark, it looks even more spectacular.

First, take the train from Düsseldorf to Duisburg, and then from there take bus 903 to *the Tiger & Turtle* stop.

Where to stay in Düsseldorf

For the best views: **25 hours hotels Düsseldorf das Tour**

This design hotel (www.25hours-hotels.com/hotels/duesseldorf/das-tour) offers stylish rooms where you immediately feel at home or wish your own bedroom looked like this. I was thrilled by the view. Whether from the inviting bar

on the top floor with a terrace, from the restaurant The Paris Club, from your own room (with bathtub on the balcony), or the wellness area, you have the whole city in view and can enjoy the skyline of Düsseldorf. Another highlight was the modern, Finnish sauna, in which you could make fragrant infusions, and also from there you had a fabulous view. For me, this was the best sauna in a city hotel so far, as it was not just a dark room, but a beautiful glass cabin. As the icing on the cake, all the food at breakfast was of the best quality and there were even oysters.

In a state-of-the-art location

The **Radisson Blu Media Harbor Hotel, Düsseldorf** (www.radissonhotels.com/de-de/hotels/radisson-blu-duesseldorf-media-harbour) is perfectly located in the modern and up-and-coming Media Harbor district. It is located a few steps from the Rhine Tower and surrounded by many inviting restaurants for all tastes. Also in the hotel itself, you will be well catered for, be it with snacks, which are available throughout the day in the lobby or at the varied breakfast buffet with à la carte options. Especially the avocado toast has won me over.

The design suite had plenty of space and in addition to the rainforest shower, there was also a huge bathtub. The bed and pillows were extremely comfortable and smelled wonderful thanks to the free relaxation spray. I slept great and would love to come back anytime!

Cologne

In Cologne, of course, the most obvious thing to notice is the imposing cathedral. The cathedral is right next to the train station and that's why it's worth getting off the train.
Cologne is also strongly connected to the Rhine and the beautiful Rhine promenade

invites you for a walk or to go cycle. Of course, a tasting of the famous Kölsch beer should not be missed. If you're here in February and the biggest carnival in the country is taking place, don't be surprised if you never get to see your hotel room because you're out partying on the streets. If you even managed to get a room with all those visitors...

From the airport to the city center

Cologne/Bonn Airport (CGN) is served by international and domestic flights. You can easily get to the city center with the S13 or the RE8 in 14 or 11 minutes for 2.70 EUR.

However, you should be careful when using trams or suburban trains in Cologne. Sometimes the entrance is offset one meter and then suddenly a staircase is folded down. If you don't pay attention to this and are standing in the entrance area, you could fall out. A friendly local saved me and my stroller from crashing at the last minute...:/

Things to do in Cologne

Cologne has diverse neighborhoods and you could well extend your stay here and explore everything in detail. However, you can also visit the main sights in one day.

It is worth paying a visit to the **tourist information** in front of the cathedral at the beginning. There you will find heaps of advertising brochures, which always contain good offers. You can also buy a **Kölncard**. It has the price and function of a normal 24h public transport ticket (9 EUR). However, you also get up to 50% discount at almost all important sights. The purchase pays off quickly because for some sights you would otherwise have to walk several kilometers (which of course also has its charm along the Rhine).

See the cathedral from all angles

Whether from the front, from the back, or from the inside, the cathedral is an impressive building that you should take a close look at. You can enter the church for free. Climbing the tower costs 6 EUR without a Kölncard and you can climb 533 steps to the platform at about 93 m.

The back of the cathedral is also very beautiful to look at and therefore you throw a glance over your shoulder on the way to the Hohenzollern Bridge.

Fun fact: Apparently, it's a local tradition to greet the cathedral as you pass by. With such a dignified sight, you might want to start with it too.

Visit a great art museum

Right next to the cathedral is the **Museum Ludwig** (www.museum-ludwig.de, Tue-Sun 10 a.m.-6 p.m., entrance fee without Kölncard: 11 EUR). It contains many famous paintings by the masters of modernism. Even if you aren't an art enthusiast, you will recognize paintings and names of Picasso, Robert Rauschenberg, Andy Warhol, and Niki de Saint

Phalle. I loved this large collection and would even call it my new favorite museum in Europe.

If you are interested in more art or if you prefer to visit the old masters from the Middle Ages to Impressionism, you will find beautiful paintings by Monet, Renoir, Rubens, Rembrandt, and much more in the **Wallraf-Richartz Museum** (www.wallraf.museum, Tue-Sun 10 a.m.-6 p.m., admission without Kölncard 13 EUR). It also had an interesting exhibition of letters and illustrations.

Walk along the Rhine promenade toward the Kranhäuser

Both banks of the Rhine are suitable for this. From the Deutz shore side you can enjoy a great view of the cathedral and the crane houses. On the city center side you can eventually stroll through the modern customs harbor. In addition, you will pass the **Chocolate Museum**, which is also an architecturally nice building from the outside. The chocolate used in the museum comes from Lindt and therefore there is also a Lindt shop at the entrance. If you like chocolate, you will certainly enjoy this visit, because where else in Germany do you have the opportunity to taste Swiss chocolate from a fountain? Admission without the Kölncard is 13.50 EUR (open daily from 10 a.m. to 6 p.m. but closed on Mondays in November and from January to the end of March).

Cross the Rhine on a bridge or by cable car

The **Hohenzollern Bridge** made of steel right next to the main train station is beautiful to look at and could also be somewhere in New York. From the Museum Ludwig, a ramp leads to the bridge, and you can cross the Rhine along thousands of love locks. Or do you even want to attach your own lock as a souvenir? On the other side is the **Triangle Tower**. For 5 EUR you can take the elevator up to the viewing platform, from where you have a fabulous view over the Cologne skyline, including the cathedral.

If a bridge is too boring for you, you also have the opportunity to cross the Rhine with a colorful cable car. Take the S18 to the *Zoo/Flora* stop, where the entrance to the **Rhine cable car** is located. From the small cabins, you have a whole new view of the water and the skyline of Cologne. In 5 minutes, you are on the other side of the river. A trip costs 5 EUR and a return ticket costs 9 EUR.

I find it a bit unfavorable that the cable car leads directly over the *Claudius Therme*. It is said to be a very nice thermal bath with many varied saunas. However, you can look down on the naked people from the cable car, which would personally disturb me when going to the sauna.

Discover free art

At the same stop as the Rhine cable car is also the sculpture park. I was expecting some small statues of wine gods or girls with braids and was surprised that it was a park filled with varied art installations that you would otherwise find in a museum. All this for free. Hence, the walk or the journey with the S-Bahn from the center here is always worthwhile, also because of the next sight.

Enjoy nature in the Botanical Garden

To get to the *Flora Park*, you pass the entrance of the zoo. Some enclosures are designed in such a way that you can catch a glimpse of the animals from the outside without entering the zoo.

In the Botanical Garden, you find beautiful fountain installations and many inviting places to sit down. If I ever have a large piece of land, I will want to hire the gardener who designed this garden. There also is an area with dahlias and other beautiful flowers and herbs. Access to the tropical house is also free. As a local, I would probably be in this garden all the time.

Visit Michael Schumacher's Motorworld

Another free attraction is the private racing car and classic car collection of Michael Schumacher. Stroll around in the two-story hall between the expensive cars and look at Ferraris, with which Schumacher has won many titles. The trophies are also on display. If you

like nice or fast cars, you should definitely come here! For everyone else, there is a playground right in front of the Motorworld or an IKEA a few minutes' walk away.

Stroll along Schildergasse to the Belgian Quarter

Back in the city center, if you still have time, you can now go on a shopping tour. The most famous shops can be found along Schildergasse. Look up at the Neumarkt, then your eyes will get stuck on a huge, overturned ice cone.

Even if you don't want to buy anything, you should visit the large *Globetrotter* store. In the basement, they have a pool where kayaks and other water sports equipment can be tried. The path continues along *Aachenerstrasse*, where there are several restaurants for every taste and finally you end up in a café or bar in the Belgian Quarter.

Where to stay in Cologne

At **the 25hours Hotel The Circle** (www.25hours-hotels.com/ hotels/koeln/the-circle) you can take off into space. Already in the lobby with the large coworking area, you feel like on a spaceship. However, the room with a view of the cathedral was very cozy and bright. It had practical gadgets such as a Bluetooth speaker, a free minibar, and many booklets that make travel hearts beat faster. If you have time after sightseeing or work, you can make yourself comfortable with a book in the beautiful sauna area or power through your own program in the pretty fitness room. The location of the hotel is central and well connected to public transport. In addition, the architecture is really worth seeing and even if you are not staying at the hotel, you could stop by the Monkey Bar for a drink on the top floor or eat something at the NENI restaurant. Breakfast was delicious, with plenty of options for meat eaters, vegetarians, and vegans.

Adina Apartment Hotel Cologne

This apartment hotel (www.adinahotels.com/de/apartments/cologne/) is especially convenient for exhibitors or visitors to the trade fair in Cologne, as the hotel is located right in front of the entrance gates. On the other side of the hotel, you have the Deutz train station, from which you can reach Cologne Cathedral in 3 minutes.

I was welcomed with a lemonade and Haribo gummy bears. The rooms are spacious and, in addition to the bed, you have a couch and an additional living area with a dining table, a comfortable leather bench, and a chair. Families or long-term travelers can look forward to a small kitchenette and an in-room washer/dryer. The fitness room is also large and variously equipped and if you still haven't done enough sports, you can swim a few lengths in the pool or relax in the Finnish sauna.

There are plenty of restaurants to choose from both in and around the hotel.

Hamburg

I always like to return to Hamburg, the beautiful Hanseatic city on the Elbe. Be it for a good musical, delicious seafood at the fish market or just to stroll through the streets and discover yet another pretty corner in this city.

How to get from the airport to the city center

The fastest and cheapest way is by S-Bahn. The stop is located just below the airport terminals. The journey between the airport (HAM) and the city center takes about 20 minutes and costs 3.60 EUR.

If you arrive or depart by cruise ship, you are lucky that the port is located in the middle of the city and you can start visiting the sights right away.

If you want to watch the big ships, you have the opportunity to do so from the *Docklands* office building. The parallelogram-like building with many windows looks like a ship itself. You can enter the roof terrace via 140 steps for free and have a great view over the waterways.

Things to do in Hamburg

Historic sights and modern architecture go hand in hand in Hamburg. You can relax on one of the beaches along the Elbe or in the park *Planten and Blomen*. The hip Schanzenviertel, HafenCity, and Jungfernstieg are also worth a visit. At night, the Reeperbahn offers all sorts of entertainment options from musicals to pub crawls. So, there is always something to experience in Hamburg.

Fill your belly with Hamburg's culinary diversity

The **fish** market is Hamburg's most famous market. It is something for partygoers who need a snack before going to bed or for fish lovers who manage to get out of bed on Sunday mornings between 5 and 9.30 a.m. (mid-March to mid-November) and from 7 to 9.30 a.m. (in the winter months). The wide range of fresh fish, crabs and clams, exotic goods, and delicious snacks is worth the effort.

For night markets you don't have to travel all the way to Thailand. Every Wednesday from March to September from 4 p.m. to 11 p.m. the **St. Pauli Night Market** takes place. From October to November, the hustle and bustle on Spielbudenplatz runs from 4 p.m. to 10 p.m. You will find fresh food of good quality, food stalls, and live music.

On the same square, a street food market with food trucks takes place every Thursday evening. In winter from 6 p.m. to 10 p.m. and in summer from 5 p.m. to 11 p.m.

If you prefer to stay indoors, you can pay a visit to the **Chocoversum**. It is an interactive chocolate experience world where visitors learn everything about the popular sweet food: from the cultivation of cocoa beans to the production of various chocolate products. During the 90-minute tour, you can taste several products and decorate your own chocolate bar at the end. Online you can book the tour starting at 19 EUR at the early bird price (https://chocoversum.de).

Another stop for pleasure lovers is the **Braugasthaus Altes Mädchen** (Lagerstraße 28B). In this brewery, you have over 30 different craft beers to choose from. Of course, there are also other drinks, and, on the menu, you find delicious councilor food: http://altes-maedchen.com/de/getraenke/.

For a delicious drink with a great view, head to the **Skylinebar 20UP** at the Empire Riverside Hotel. At 90 meters you have a fabulous view over the harbor and the Elbe through the huge windows.

Visit the architectural masterpieces

Let's start with the **Elbphilharmonie** (Platz d. Deutschen

Einheit 4), which is one of the most modern, innovative, and spectacular concert halls in the world. It is at the top of Hamburg's skyline and offers 2,000 seats, eight different concert halls, and a panoramic view over the port city. Access to the observation deck "The Plaza" costs 2 EUR and is open daily from 10 a.m. to midnight. In addition to the fact that you can see the imposing architecture up close, you also have a good view of the harbor and the ships.

Another modern building worth seeing is the **Unilever House** (Strandkai 1) or the **Chilehaus** (Fischertwiete 2) which was modeled after a ship with its pointed edges.

If you prefer historic buildings, you should pay a visit to the Hamburg **City Hall**. The Renaissance building is richly decorated with busts and statues.

Finally, you will also notice the main church of St. Michaelis, affectionately called **Michel**.

While many parts of Hamburg were bombed during the Second World War, the church tower survived this chapter unscathed. You can climb the tower up to a viewing platform at 83 m over 452 steps (8 EUR) or take an elevator for part of the way.

The **main church of St. Nikolai** on Hamburg's Hopfenmarkt did not survive the war so unscathed. Instead of renovating the church, the building structure was secured so that the church could remain as a memorial.

Walk through the Speicherstadt

Speicherstadt Hamburg is a UNESCO World Heritage Site and one of the most important areas for trade and goods storage in all of Europe. It was planned and built in 1888 by the free traders to enable the rapid unloading of ships. The neighborhood consists of hundreds of warehouses, all stylishly decorated and built along the Elbe River.

Have fun on the Reeperbahn

Since the 19th century, the Reeperbahn has been the place where nightclubs, bars, and clubs of all kinds can be found. It has always been the heart of the entertainment district of St. Pauli with its countless attractions for young and old. There are also many musical theaters, cinemas, and venues for all tastes, as well as a variety of culinary delights. So, even if you may have heard that it is the largest red light district in Europe, don't let that stop you from visiting the Reeperbahn. The most famous red-light street is *Herbertstraße*. In the 1970s, a sign was put up saying "Access forbidden to young people under 18 and women" because they wanted to maintain the moral order. However, there is no legal foundation and anyone who wants can enter this street.

Go shopping

The **Alsterarkaden** shine in Venetian beauty and form the oldest shopping arcade in Hamburg. In a classic ambiance along the river, there are exclusive fashion shops, the finest jewelry shops, and boutiques with individual gift ideas.

If you prefer it modern, you should go to the most famous shopping street in the city; the **Neuer Wall** shopping street. On more than 10,000 square meters you will find everything your heart desires.

Follow in the footsteps of the Beatles

The Beatles-Platz in Hamburg is a place of music history. The square was named after John Lennon, Paul McCartney, George Harrison, and Ringo Starr in 2008. It is reminiscent of the time when the Beatles had their first big success in Germany – above all, of course, with their appearances in the Star Club. The square is visited by fans from all over the world. On the Beatles Square, there are regular concerts, and you have the opportunity to listen to the echoes of the past. In addition, a guitar and four drumsticks are embedded in the floor. A must - not only for fans of the quartet!

Relax in a park

Planten un Blomen is one of the most beautiful parks in

Germany. It is located right in the heart of the city and gives its visitors the feeling of being in the middle of a green oasis. The park extends over more than fifty hectares and is home to numerous attractive sights, such as the Japanese Garden, the Park Theater, or the fountain on the park lake. In summer, this fountain turns into a water show several times a day (2 p.m., 4 p.m., and 6 p.m.). 10 p.m. (in September at 21 p.m.) the spectacle is additionally accompanied by light and music.

If you are in Hamburg with children, you should stop at **Grasbrookpark**. Right near the Unilever building, there is a great playground in this park.

Visit the first zoo with animal enclosures without bars

What is common practice for animal-friendly zoos today all began in Tierpark Hagenbeck (https://hagenbeck.de), when Carl Hagenbeck patented outdoor animal facilities without bars. In the zoo, you will encounter a fascinating variety of animal inhabitants – from giraffes to lions to walruses. The entrance fee for adults only for the zoo is 29 EUR, for the aquarium 25 EUR, and for both together 45 EUR.

Walk along the Elbe or take a dip

Along the Elbe, there is a nice path, on which you could walk from the city center to the **Elbe beach Övelgönne** in 20 minutes. From there you have a great view of the harbor from a distance and can enjoy a cooling swim in the Elbe in summer. At the *Ahoy beach kiosk* or at the *Restaurant Strandperle* you can eat something if you have not brought anything for a barbecue.

If you do not want to walk, you can also take *boat line 62* from the Landungsbrücken in the direction of *Neumühlen* to the Elbe beach.

Mallorcan holiday feeling can be found in the *28-degree lido* (Hakendamm 2, 22880 Wedel).

See Hamburg from a different perspective and take a boat trip

In Hamburg, you don't have to buy an expensive port cruise to enjoy a trip on the water. The river is used as a normal public transport road and the HADAG ferries only cost a normal public transport ticket. With line 62 you can pass all the places worth seeing along the Elbe in Hamburg.

Celebrate with Hamburg

Three times a year, Northern Germany's largest fair takes place in Hamburg. On the Spring Dom, Summer Dom, or Winter Dom you will find rides and food stalls. Fireworks are also held.

An even bigger festival is the Hafengeburtstag (port birthday), which takes place annually in May over a weekend. There are many attractions along the water, around the ships, and again a big fireworks display.

A Day Trip from Hamburg to Lüneburg

Lüneburg is a medieval town in northern Germany known for its beautiful buildings. The city was already an important trading center in the Middle Ages and is still rich in architectural monuments from this time.

How to get to Lüneburg

In 30 to 50 minutes, you can get from Hamburg directly to Lüneburg by train, starting from 12.90 EUR.

A city tour in Lüneburg

From the train station, our first destination is the **crane in the port of Lüneburg**. On the other side of the river Ilmenau is the pretty **Stintmarkt**, whose houses are worth some photos. If you are already hungry or thirsty, you can sit on the terrace directly at the water and look at the old salt barges, because Lüneburg was once the salt stronghold of the Hansen.

Nearby is the beautiful **St. Nicolai Church.** It is worth seeing both from the outside and from the inside. Then stroll past the town **hall** through the

historic old town towards the market square **Am Sande**, where many other historic houses and inviting cafés are lined up. Refueled again, we continue to the **water tower**. It was built in the 19th century as waterworks for agriculture and is still considered a landmark of the city. From its platform, you have a breathtaking view over the rooftops of the market and the adjacent river. The entrance fee is 5 EUR.

The last attraction that you should not miss is the **Salt Museum** (Sülfmeisterstraße 1, 21335 Lüneburg, Tue to Sun 10 a.m. – 5 p.m.). In an interactive exhibition, you can learn more about the history of salt mining. The entrance fee is 8 EUR. With the buses 5003, 5007, or 5011 you can get back to the station.

International connections from Germany

Without Covid restrictions, it is very easy to enter Germany's neighboring countries.

Germany borders Switzerland, France, Luxembourg, Belgium, the Netherlands, Denmark, Poland, the Czech Republic, and Austria. So, you have endless possibilities to combine your trip with these countries, depending on which region of Germany you are currently in. From Dusseldorf, you are in Amsterdam in 2h 20min with the ICE. From Konstanz you are in Zurich in 1h 15min.

About the author of this guidebook

Seraina / SwissMiss OnTour has loved to travel for as long as she can remember. It started with beach holidays with her family in Mallorca when she was a child, but soon she was looking for her own routes. She was lucky to spend a fabulous High School year in New York at the age of 15. It was at this point that she began writing her first travel blog, from which *SwissMissOnTour.com* evolved. Later she explored Europe with

Interrail but was also attracted by the exotic countries further away. Countless trips to Southeast Asia led her to fall in love with the delicious Asian flavors, beautiful temples, and nature. She always had South America in the back of her mind, but she wanted to have more time to avoid having to fly back and forth to Switzerland every holiday. When the timing was right, she quit her job and enjoyed the countries of South America to the fullest. Unfortunately, the coronavirus pandemic has forced her to return to Switzerland earlier than planned. Here she once again takes every opportunity to explore places near and far. Another exciting adventure began in 2022 when her daughter was born. Since Seraina also traveled quite a bit during her pregnancy and now with the baby, feel free to contact her on Instagram if you have any questions or concerns about travel during pregnancy or with small children.

Book your hotel stays through me

I now have access to better booking conditions for hotel stays and flights. As an introductory offer, if you book three or more nights through me, you can choose one of my travel guide e-books for free. Just contact me at swissmissontour@gmail.com and send your accommodation dates, your desired hotel or the city of the accommodation, and your budget.

Some useful words in German

English	German
Hello	Hallo
How are you doing?	Wie geht es dir?
I am well and you?	Mir geht es gut und dir?
Where are you from?	Woher kommst du?
I come from...	Ich komme aus… (den USA, England, Australien)
Yes	Ja
No	Nein
Please, write it down.	Bitte, schreibe es auf.
Where is the toilet/ATM?	Wo ist das WC / der Bankomat?
Thank you very much.	Vielen Dank
How much is...?	Wie viel kostet…?
I'm sorry	Es tut mir leid.
Please	Bitte
I need to change money.	Ich möchte Geld wechseln.
I would like...	Ich hätte gerne…
The bill, please.	Die Rechnung, bitte.
Water	Wasser
Chicken	Hühnchen
without meat	Ohne Fleisch
Enjoy your meal.	Guten Appetit
When is ...?	Wo ist…?
Bus	Bus
Airplane	Flugzeug
Boat	Schiff / Boot
Waterfall	Wasserfall
Right	Rechts
Left	Links
Straight on	Gerade aus

Do you need more information?

In case you need more information or want to book your accommodation through me, I am happy to help. Contact or follow me through the following channels.
Especially on Instagram I am active and post daily travel inspiration, tips or travel quotes.

(b) www.swissmissontour.com

(i) @swissmissontour

(f) SwissMissOnTour

(w) www.slgigerbooks.wordpress.com

(@) swissmissontour@gmail.com

Did you like this travel guide?

In case you liked this travel guide, I'd greatly appreciate a positive review on Amazon, and it would be a good support if you told your friends about it 😊
Scan the QR-code to leave your review.

Your free download

Never forget anything important ever again and don't waste unnecessary time with packing. Scan the QR code and receive a free packing list along with a sample of my Thailand travel guide.

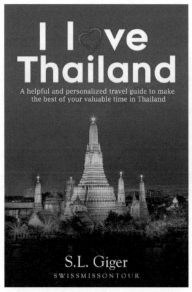

Your Travel Journal

Scan the QR-code to download a stunning travel diary, crafted to lovingly capture the cherished moments and unforgettable souvenirs from your travels.

More books by S. L. Giger / SwissMiss OnTour

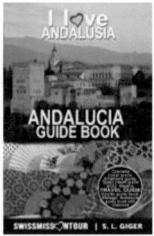
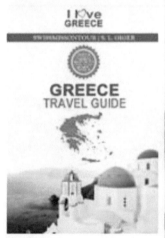

And many more. Check the books out on Amazon.

Manufactured by Amazon.ca
Bolton, ON